The Messiah

Immortalised in Time

Michael Hearns

Copyright © The Messiah Immortalised in Time,

Michael Hearns, 2017

All rights reserved: no part of this publication may be reproduced, stored in a retrieval system, or transmitted in any form or by any means, electronic, mechanical, photocopying or otherwise without the prior written permission of the publisher.

ISBN 978-0-9930591-2-4

Revised 1st October 2023

Self-Published in Dublin, Ireland.

The moral right of the author has been asserted

A copy of the CIP entry for this book is available from

The Copyright Library of Congress, Washington DC, USA

And Trinity College Dublin, Ireland.

www.sevenbiblewonders.com

Table of Contents

Introduction 1

Chapter 1 The Prophecies of a Messiah 10

Chapter 2 The Secret Calendar Archive 18

Chapter 3 The Incredible Old Ages were in fact Time Periods 27

Chapter 4 Reconstructing the Biblical calendar 31

Chapter 5 The Reed-777 Day Formula............................ 39

Chapter 6 The Messiah Immortalised in Time 43

Chapter 7 The Heaven on Earth Configuration of the Tabernacle... 80

Chapter 8 The Resurrection through the Lens of the Tabernacle.. 107

Conclusion 115

Appendix 1: Mercury, Seven Years and Peace Offerings 123

Bibliography 127

Tables

Table 1: The Days of a Solar Calendar……………..……..……23

Table 2: The Days of a Strategic Solar Calendar in the Fourth Chart ………………………..…………..……..25

Table 3: The Incredible Ages compare to the Converted periods of the Calendar …………………………28

Table 4: The Orbits of the Planets and Time periods in the Tabernacle Dimensions ………………..…..81

Diagrams

Diagram 1: The Sponsors stand over Five Tribes 35

Diagram 2: The Messiah Calendar Timeline in the 4th Chart 36

Diagram 3: The Conception and Births of John and Jesus 52

Diagram 4: The Shape of a Divining Rod 66

Diagram 5: The Complete Picture with the Messiah Timeline 73

Diagram 6: The Dazzling Reflection of the Rising Sun from the Golden Walls and Ornaments of the Tabernacle 92

Diagram 7: The Lunar Month of 29.5 Days in the Surface Areas of the Ark and Incense Altar 93

Diagram 8: The Orbit of Mars in the Surface areas of the Tabernacle Tent and its Furniture 94

Diagram 9: The Orbit of Mercury in the Square Areas of the Holiest Chamber and its Furniture 95

Diagram 10: The Solar Year in the Surface Areas of the Holiest Chamber and the Seat and Breastplate .. 96

Diagram 11: The Period of 5,108 Days in the Square Areas of Perimeter, Outer Room and Furniture 98

Diagram 12: The Special Cycle of Saturn at 383 Years ... 99

Introduction

The central thesis of this investigation is that the coming of the predicted Messiah was promoted by painstaking planning on a projected sacred timeline. It can now be shown that the prophets undertook the biggest PR initiative in the history of mankind in order to announce the coming of the Messiah. Nothing was left to chance. The epiphany was plotted with systematic brilliance using mathematical wizardry. Provision was made for a golden circle of chosen people to feature beginning with the father figure Abraham.

The timing was mapped out along a sacred timeline using red letter dates and time spans within which, a pantheon of biblical superstars were introduced. The choreography of each new arrival was prepared with the same painstaking effort used today to build up the profiles of celebrity VIPs. In contemporary parlance, the scribes took on the role of promoters and their key projection was with the forecast of a Messiah. Some fifty five generations would eventually complete the family tree rooted in the work of those who devised the route map to the Messiah.

The prophets had somehow attained a sophisticated knowledge of the heavens, which was charted on secret calendars with remarkable intricacy. These calendars were used to calculate dates centuries into the future and it is now decoded here for the first time. This alternative story is not one of serpents and saints but on hard facts based on detailed scientific analysis. Simply put, all the milestones laid along the path for the Redeemer were devised to

Introduction

authenticate his arrival at the end of days. Behind the scenes the elite circle employed secret calendars of almost impossible complexity which gave them the power of determination. They watched the heavens and had acquired the ability to forecast with total accuracy the unfolding of cosmic momentous events.

Working on the basis that facts are sacred, this book follows a series of earthly and astronomical signposts that were laid down secretly in the Book of Numbers and in other parts of the Bible. These signposts literally take you on a walk through the heavens, the realm of the gods. The prophets set down a pathway using the building blocks of numbers by which they could follow in the footsteps of the lord. From Jacob's ladder, the endeavor to scale the heavens if only in a dream, to the beguiling Tower of Babel, the aspiration of mortals was to soar up to the Almighty. The workers on the fantastical tower, we are told spoke one language though they reputedly came from the four corners of the earth. What could that one language have been? Strangely, the answer is relatively simple for the language of construction workers is in numbers and measurements. Yes, it was the one true language of mathematics.

The Bible is fundamentally the most celebrated S.O.S signal in the history of humanity. It will be shown that the scribes used their extraordinary understanding of the heavens to construct a bridge to infinity and thus achieve the divine attribute of immortality in the metaphorical sense. Their message was the most important ever communicated for it was no less than the word of the one true God that they adored. It is far from fanciful to suggest that they might, given their ability with numbers, transmit part of their message through science a far more lucid and direct medium than the ambiguity of words.

The prophets had two calendar systems to map out the biblical history timeline, one of which was applied in years while the other applied in days. This secret timeline was weighted with calculated significance. The 24 hours in the day, the seven days in the week and the 365 days through which the earth travels around the sun were the fragments of this timeline. Step by step a cogent case emerged to suggest that by analyzing in isolation the verbal content of the Bible, the message and significance of the numerical dimension has been lost sight of.

Cynics will immediately scoff: Is it credible that primitive goat herders and shepherds who relied upon the technology of the abacus to count their very flocks could actually compute on a par with modern science? Let's remind ourselves that time has been the most tangent link between mortals and the heavens for millennia. Divine connections were made with the sun as day and the moon as night – light and darkness, good and evil. That journey around the sun has had a sacred significance before the hourglass or sundials were ever devised.

Not since Samson flexed the full span of his mighty arms to bring the temple crashing down, have the pillars of conventional belief been so sorely tested. But this endeavor is not about sacking the temple, though it will certainly annul some of the myths and practices that religious establishments have rested on for thousands of years. In their place however the findings do unveil the format of a magnificent numerical sophistication in all its multi-layered ingeniousness. The revelation that some of the most beautiful lyrical parables of the Bible as well as some of its most disturbing texts carried a watermark that can only be seen when held up to the light of physics and science may seem controversial at first. But the clues were there nonetheless. What was required was a pains taking analysis of the numbers based on detailed calculations.

The ingenuity of the timeline lay in the fact that it empowered the cognoscenti. It was used to lay down a red carpet on the biblical highway along which a selection of heavyweights would walk. By the time they entered the story the audience would be prepared for their arrival by the confluence of special indicators, signs or portents. These were generally celestial and created a sense of divine connection. It imbued the character with a mystique or aura. It culminated with the birth of Jesus Christ, and his receipt of the royal ointment from the Magi.

One of the calendars included the indices that identified the Star of Bethlehem as the two planets of Jupiter and Saturn coming very close together three times in the year 7 BCE. In turn, the data suggested that Jesus was likely born on the 26th February in the year 6 BCE.

These new discoveries may sound astonishing but they shed light on a secret biblical conspiracy, which was only detected by scholars in recent centuries. In this investigation I learned that the earliest books of the Bible had been covertly re-edited several hundred years before Jesus. In the re-editing process such stories as the exodus and the flood epic had been hyped up into Hollywood type sagas. Interestingly, the re-editing involved the insertion of volumes of mysterious domestic related numbers into scripture including practically the whole Book of Numbers.[1] It was a daring exercise for instead of safeguarding the numerical data in a vault or caves, they literally placed the information in the Bible where it lay hidden in plain sight.

The analysis shows that the writers repackaged the original data of the heavens and inserted it as domestic related issues such as with the incredible ages of the patriarchs or as the unbelievable population sizes of men who wandered through the desert wilderness. Those two huge population sizes would have won Oscars for pretending to be men in censuses simply because nobody had ever challenged the farcical listings with their

---

[1] Reference Richard Elliot Friedman, Who Wrote the Bible? New York: Harper, 1997

numbers. Those listings of men in the census tallies all ended with the unit's digit of zero. It must be the first written example of fake news because any census tally would end with an even distributions of the numbers between zero, one, two etc. up to nine. The analysis will show that the numbers that were paraded as men in two censuses were instead the days of a sophisticated solar calendar.

The disguise worked and the indices of the solar calendar timeline went undetected where they lay hidden before our eyes in the most scrutinized book in history. Some of the numbers became the subject of ghoulish entertainment where they were exploited by eccentrics trying to predict the end is nigh. But at last, the great secret knowledge is out in the open and there for all to view. However, people will wonder why did the writers not place the celestial data on open display in the Bible?

The answer to the perplexing puzzle would suggest that it was to preserve privileged information such as sacred numerical data on astronomy, which the priests had somehow acquired from antiquity. Knowledge was power and so the data could not be shared with the masses or let fall into the hands of hostile nations. Yet the knowledge had to be preserved and passed on in case the elite few perished. In those ancient times, education and writing was limited to royalty and the priests. Oral tradition was the societal norm and story-telling was perhaps the greatest memory aid to safeguard knowledge from the past.

In a book named Hamlet Mill, the authors had researched this subject on how ancient myths were likely to have been encoded with astronomical knowledge of the heavens.[2] The book was criticized for lack of solid evidence and was viewed as flashes of insights by the authors into the

---

[2] Hamlets Mill Giorgio De Santillana, Hertha von Dechend, David R. Publisher Godine, 1977

cyclical world of the ancients and the nature of mythical language. But now from antiquity the evidence will be produced to reveal the indices of astronomy, which slumbered in the Bible.

The purpose of the cosmic data was to lay out the sacred timeline for the coming of a Messiah. This anointed one was understood to be God sending a powerful leader like David or Solomon who would restore the Jews to their past glory. Such a liberator may have been on the minds of the prophets who witnessed the oppression of their brethren first hand. But the seers had another agenda to promote and it was in the realms of the divine. The evidence suggests that their agenda was to try and ease the shocking finality of death with its terrible trauma for the departing souls and their grieving families. We were led to believe by the Bible that God would send his only son on a formidable divine mission here on earth, which would revolutionize civilizations whole existence. This Messiah would preach of love and justice, heal the sick and spread peace throughout the land. But his foremost mission was to open up a gateway to heaven in the afterlife so that mortals could avoid the clutches of the grim reaper lurking at the graveside.

Heretofore, there were just two main points of view to explain the prophecies of a Messiah and the mission of Jesus. On the one hand there were the religious followers who believed that the prophets were divinely inspired and that Jesus was the son sent by God to open up the kingdom of heaven to the faithful. The faithful could readily accept that Jesus changed water into wine, walked on water and raised Lazarus from the dead for with God such miracles were possible. To sceptics however, the Messiah was a self-fulfilling prophecy and the gospel writers had invoked snippets of the predictions to justify that Jesus was the anointed one. This last point was borne out where the Jews do not accept that Jesus was the predicted Messiah. We read in the gospels that the Pharisees often challenged Jesus on points of law or customs. If there were such miracles for them to observe, why then were they not also mesmerized by them?

Because of the research findings, those two different points of view are now under challenge because neither the Christian churches nor the Jewish congregation knew about the sacred Messiah timeline. That sacred timeline will greatly impact on the predictions of a Messiah and pose many questions. For instance, how could the prophets know that a Saviour would be born at the time of an unusual star and that his birthplace would be Bethlehem especially as they lived at least five hundred years beforehand? This is where the sacred timeline is invaluable. Not only was Jesus in the right place Bethlehem, but the timeline shows that he was also there at the right time to be the predicted Messiah.

The discoveries continued when a wonderful knowledge of the heavens was detected in the holy tabernacle. The tabernacle was one of the most holy shrines of the Hebrews and it housed the iconic Ark of the Covenant. While studying the measurements and instructions to build the tabernacle I noticed that three of the gold and silver weights listed to decorate the structure had the same numerical values as three heavenly orbits. Because the numerical values related to the weight of gold and silver, the lure of a treasure trail beckoned. I followed that treasure trail by examining the dimensions of the tabernacle and its iconic furniture for evidence of further time periods. The investigation proved to be revolutionary for I found that the various dimensions of the tabernacle in the biblical units of square cubits had the same numerical values as the orbits of the planets and other related time periods.

Initially it seemed to me that the tabernacle designers had been overzealous with the design features when they

Introduction

factored in the heavenly orbits. However, the cosmic data overlaid on the dimensions of the tabernacle changed the perception of the sacred structure from an earthly building of wooden boards and curtains into a metaphysical heavenly dominion. This enhanced the image of the tabernacle and made it a suitable setting to explain the transition from this earthly world into a metaphysical world in heaven. It was the evidence that opened up a new window into the resurrection of Jesus. The findings indicate that the gospel writers had used the holy tabernacle as an image for the tomb in order to present the resurrection of Jesus in heaven and earthly setting. This explained why it outlined in the gospels that the veil of the temple or tabernacle was rent in two when Jesus died because it joined the outer holy chamber that symbolized earth to the inner chamber that symbolized heaven.

The prophecies of a Messiah were scattered over many books in the Old Testament and were therefore difficult to access. But in this book those prophecies are summed up in a few pages. The quest initially begins by investigating the prophesies, which were referred to in the gospels at the birth of Jesus. However, the words of those prophecies were ambiguous enough to be open to different interpretations depending on the standpoint of the religious reader.

There was also the case where other charismatic personalities than Jesus were considered to be the expected Messiah and thus the predictions by the prophets had been flexible enough to become self-fulfilling prophecies. It is therefore intended to quote all of the relevant prophecies from the Old Testament and look at them from a neutral standpoint to see what the prophets actually wrote. As the investigation progressed it became evident that the prophecies not only predicted the coming of a Messiah but they also gave clues and hints that led to a secret archive where a sacred calendar lay hidden in plain sight disguised as two censuses. Step by step the evidence emerged to show that the prophets had used the secret calendar to map out a sacred timeline, which charted the history of the Jewish people from Abraham down to the predicted Messiah.

Chapter 1

The Prophecies of a Messiah

Most of the biblical prophets emerged as a *tour de force* on the biblical horizon sometime after the ninth century BCE and they played a fundamental role in shaping righteous thinking. Those visionaries were perceived to be divinely inspired and they acted with an independent voice. Instead of commanding armies with weapons, the prophets stood alone and wielded power by a higher almighty force. They were deemed to have the power to predict the future of the Jews together with the activities or demise of their enemies.

The greatest prophecy in the Old Testament was of the coming of a Messiah and snippets of the forecasts were evident with several of the prophets. As a result, the Jews could have been continually on the lookout for this expected Messiah and a close watch kept looking for signs that would identify him relative to the details the prophets had forecast. So, when Jesus came the gospels recorded the fulfillment of several predictions of the Messiah beginning with Matthew's gospel where he outlined about the arrival of the Magi.

The Magi came enquiring from King Herod and asked him: *"Where is he that is born King of the Jews? For we have seen his star in the east and have come to worship him."* [3] This was a strange introduction to the very first page of the New Testament for the Magi had

---

[3] Matthew Chapter 2:2

introduced the subject of Astrology into the scene where they said they had seen the star of the king of the Jews. Herod consulted with the priests and they referred to a prediction by a prophet named Balaam back at the time of Moses. Balaam had predicted the coming of a ruler and he had linked the event to a star where he stated: *"A star will come out of Jacob a sceptre will rise out of Israel... A ruler will come out of Jacob."*[4] Thus, the gospel statement had encapsulated the words of Balaam in the dialogue with Herod and the Magi.

The prophet Micah identified the place of the Messiah's birth where he stated: *"But you o Bethlehem, in the land of Judah, are by no means least among the rulers of Judah; for out of you will come a ruler who will be the shepherd of my people Israel."*[5] The quote built on the earlier prediction by Balaam about a ruler but the prophet Micah went on and identified the place of origin of the Messiah as Bethlehem and of course Jesus was born in Bethlehem.

Isaiah was the next prophet in line and his unusual prediction stated: *"Therefore the Lord himself shall give you a sign; Behold, a virgin shall conceive, and bear a son, and shall call his name Im-man-u-el."*[6] This prophecy was accepted as Isaiah having predicted a Messiah who would be born of a virgin. I have since read that there was a mistranslation and that the word 'virgin' was cited instead of the original Hebrew Bible wording with *"a woman shall conceive."*

After the Magi had visited Jesus, they were told in a dream to go home by a different route so as to avoid alerting King Herod of the whereabouts of the infant child. When Herod realized that he was duped he ordered the

---

[4] Book of Number's Chapter 24: 17.19
[5] Matthew Chapter 2:6, Book of Micah Chapter 5:2
[6] Book of Isaiah Chapter 7:14

massacre of all new born boys in order to eliminate a contender for his throne. It was usually interpreted that this foul act by Herod caused Matthew to invoke a prophecy from Jeremiah as follows: ***"Rachel weeping for her children, and would not be comforted, because they are not."*** [7] Rachel was the wife of the founding father of the Israelites who was named Jacob and the couple formed a central part of the earliest Jewish family genealogy. Jacob was the patriarch of the twelve tribes of Israel and his name featured in Balaam's prophecy.

Traditional sources had interpreted Rachel's weeping as being her spirit crying for the baby victims of Herod's massacre of the new born baby boys. However, there were other reasons for the spirit of Rachel weeping especially because of what happened to her own two children who were Joseph and Benjamin? Her son Joseph was sold into slavery in Egypt by his own step-brothers and Rachel died in labour giving birth to her second son Benjamin. And of all places Rachel died in Bethlehem where Jesus was born.

By questioning the traditional standpoint of Jeremiah's prophecy about Rachel weeping for her children some pertinent issues came to notice. The quote had inadvertently introduced Benjamin because he was also born to Rachel at Bethlehem. After that I became aware that the names of several of Benjamin's stepbrothers were also evident at the birth and circumcision of Jesus or in other parts of the gospels. At the circumcision of Jesus there was a man called Simeon in attendance together with Anna who was identified as a descendant of the tribe of Asher. Both those names of Simeon and Asher featured as leaders of the tribes of Israel. Jesus was born unto the tribe of Judah and later in the gospels the names of Zebulun and Naphtali were cited. [8] The name of Ephraim was also cited

---

[7] Matthew Chapter 2, Jeremiah Chapter 31
[8] Matthew's Chapter 4:15:16

in the gospels where Jesus visited the city of Ephraim. [9] Those names with Simeon, Asher, Judah, Zebulun, Naphtali, Ephraim and the implied name of Benjamin were seven of the names of the twelve tribes of Israel. It made me wonder was there anything significant as to why they were specifically listed or inferred too in the gospels. The names turned out to be a coded configuration, which would identify the celestial phenomenon, which became known as the Star of Bethlehem.

The research moved on from there and I read the various prophecies in the Old Testament. I also read the adjoining text associated with the original predictions in order to try and place the forecasts in context. After all that was what a detective would do in trying to cover all of the angles in an investigation. There were several associated references which had not featured previously with Gospel commentators yet I found them thought provoking. For instance, in the adjoining text with the quote from Jeremiah about Rachel weeping for her children it stated as follows: ***"I am a father to Israel and Ephraim is my first born."*** [10] In today's language this was fake news because Ephraim was not the first born for his brother Manasseh was older than him. Even at this early stage of the investigation, I felt that this mistake was like a prospecting license to follow Ephraim and see why he was fingered out for attention by such an error.

I soon found that Isaiah's prophecy relevant to a woman shall conceive also had some unusual small print in the adjoining text with reference to Ephraim as follows: ***"Within three score and five years shall Ephraim be broken, that it be not a people."*** [11] This is where it is important to observe the body language for the period of 65

---

[9] John 11:24
[10] Book of Jeremiah Chapter 31
[11] Book of Isaiah Chapter 7:8 KJV

solar years was also the same length in days as 67 lunar years. Therefore, there was a hidden element or double meaning with Isaiah quoting the period of 65 years. It also should be noted that the first age of the patriarch Enoch was 65 years and he supposedly died when he was at the notable number of 365 years old. This number of 365 was also the number of days in the solar year and this will soon have a major bearing on the investigation.

These extra snippets seemed to be potent clues but I also wondered why had Isaiah stated *that it be not a people, which can be broken open?* The statement by Isaiah was followed later in the text where it went on to state: *"In that day, in every place where there were a thousand vines worth a thousand silver shekels."* [12] The reference to a thousand vines worth a thousand shekels had not featured previously with investigators but soon it would prove to have a deeper meaning which was numerically time related.

There was one final clue to be considered with reference to the flight into Egypt by the holy family in order to escape the slaughter by King Herod. It outlined in Matthew's gospel how this departure would in turn fulfil the prophecy from Hosea as follows: *"Out of Egypt have I called my son"* [13] I then read the original prophecy from Hosea as follows: *"When Israel was a child, then I loved him, and called my son out of Egypt.* [14] It appeared as if Matthew was using poetic license when he referenced Hosea because the association with Jesus in the prophecy was so tenuous? Instead, the prophet had named Israel as a child, which was in fact Jacob. Jacob was not in Egypt as a child so there was a need to look further to see who was the son who was called out of Egypt.

---

[12] Book of Isaiah Chapter 7:23 Revised KJV
[13] Matthew Chapter 2:15
[14] Book of Hosea Chapter 11:1

Just two sentences down from the quote in Hosea the small print in the reference continued as follows: ***"I thought Ephraim also to go, taking them by their arms; but they knew not that I healed them."*** [15] The earlier reference to Israel (Jacob) and now to Ephraim was more realistic in the quotes from Hosea because Jacob went to live in Egypt in his old age and there, he met for the first time his grandson Ephraim. The part of the phrase ***"but they knew not that I healed them"*** was interesting because to heal someone you bandage or cover up their wounds. Was this reference to *I healed them* a hint of a cover up?

The investigation continued with Luke's gospel where it outlined how Joseph and Mary went up to Bethlehem to be recorded in a census. This was not a prophecy but the citation was dynamic as Follows:

"In those days Caesar Augustus issued a decree that a census should be taken of the entire Roman world. (This was the first census that took place while Quirinius was governor of Syria.) And everyone went to their own town to register. So, Joseph also went up from the town of Nazareth in Galilee to Judea, to Bethlehem the town of David, because he belonged to the house and line of David. He went there to register with Mary, who was pledged to be married to him and was expecting a child." [16]

Even though this reference to a census was not prophesised it nevertheless has confounded biblical scholar because there was no historical evidence to support the position of a census having been held at the birth of Jesus. Why then had Luke made reference to a mysterious census, which seemingly never took place? And why was it emphasised as the *first census*?

---

[15] Book of Hosea 11:3
[16] Luke Chapter 2:1-5. NIV

Chapter 1 - The Prophecies of a Messiah

In the quotations so far, four of the prophets had singled out Rachel's grandchild Ephraim for special attention. The quest now was to check in scripture for signs of something which **can be broken with 65 years** and **that it be not a people,** with the expectation of finding **a 1,000 vines or shekels.** Included in the quest was Jeremiah's reference to **Ephraim as a young boy who is perceived to be the first born.** There were also those references from Hosea linking **Israel with Ephraim, coming out of Egypt and taking them by the arms.** There was also that reference to a first census to be investigated.

The Sign of the Cross

With those clues on board, it was easy to detect where the quote from Hosea about *Israel with Ephraim coming out of Egypt and taking them by the arms* featured. It involved a high profiled scene with Jacob, his son Joseph and two grandsons Manasseh and Ephraim, which was outlined in Chapter 48 of the Book of Genesis. In the scene, Jacob laid the groundwork where he fretfully referred to Rachel and notably how he had buried her in Bethlehem. He then sought to bless the two boys. Joseph led his two sons towards Jacob ensuring that the older Manasseh went to the right hand side and the younger Ephraim to the left hand side of their grandfather. This was necessary so that Jacob would bless the older son Manasseh with his right hand as was the traditional custom.

Things did not work out that way however because Jacob deliberately crossed his arms to bless the younger Ephraim with his right hand while he blessed the older Manasseh with his left hand. The boy's father complained to Jacob because blessing the younger Ephraim with the right hand went against tradition. However, Jacob justified his actions by stating that Ephraim would be greater than Manasseh. In effect, Jacob had made the sign of the cross by overlapping his two arms and of course the cross was to become associated with the ever lasting image of Jesus. The clues in the small print with Hosea of ***Ephraim, Israel, Egypt and taking them by the arms*** had borne fruit and remarkably, even at that early stage in biblical history, the prophets had indicated that the cross was the sign to follow.

I wanted to see what was so special about Ephraim for him to be singled out so prominently by Jacob so I employed the aid of a biblical search engine to home in on more listings of him. When I entered the name Ephraim and hit the return key the search engine stopped at Chapter 1 in the Book of Numbers. It was there that Moses had conducted a census of the twelve tribes of Israel. On a trail that had begun with the reference to an unknown first census it was spectacular to find the search had borne fruit where it had led to the first census of the twelve tribes of Israel. There was however something dreadfully wrong with the totals of the numbers in that census, which was truly astonishing and demanded a thorough investigation.

Chapter 2

The Secret Calendar Archive

We were led to believe that 603,550 men were counted by Moses in a census of the twelve tribes of Israel at the end of the first year on the exodus out of Egypt.[17] This total was unreal especially as the Bible says that there were only seventy people in total when the patriarch Jacob moved to Egypt just five generations previously.[18] A quick glance at the census figures was an eye opener where it immediately revealed that eleven of the census numbers of the twelve tribes ended with a double zero such as with Benjamin at 35,400 men. Common sense tells us that this could not have been the outcome of a census because in any tally, the numbers end with random digits distributed in unit figures from zero to nine. Therefore, the size of the alleged population size was too enormous to fit in with the storyline and also eleven of the numbers ended with the bizarre anomaly of a double zero

These peculiar observations raised an interesting question. Were the first three digits listed for each tribe multiplied by one hundred for that would account for the last two digits ending with a double zero? For instance, was the tribe of Benjamin at 35,400 men in reality numbered as 354 men? The reason for posing this question was that the three digit number at 354 men with Benjamin was also the equivalent of the number of days in a lunar year. Was that observation just a mere coincidence?

---

[17] Book of Numbers Chapter 1
[18] Book of Genesis Chapter 46:27

Had anybody in the countless millions of readers of the Bible investigated why the number may have been multiplied by one hundred? It was so glaring that I checked through the Bible to see if the scribes had anything to say about the matter. I was pleasantly surprised to find that there were two quotes where it stated that the census had been multiplied by a hundred fold. The first quote was in the second Book of Samuel where King David instructed the captain of the host, Joab, to go through all the tribes of Israel and number the people. Joab's reply was rather telling where it stated: *"Now the lord thy God add unto the people. How many so ever they be, an hundredfold, and that the eyes of my lord the king may see it;"* The story was repeated in the first Book of Chronicles where Joab's response to the king was equally telling as follows: *The lord made his people an hundred times so many more as they be:"* Both statements suggested that the numbers of the tribes were multiplied by one hundred times more.

The twelve tribes were supposed to have been the descendants of Jacob's ten sons and two grandsons. The storyline tells us that God was fed up listening to the moans of the freed slaves and declared that they would die before reaching the Promised Land of milk and honey. Therefore, a second census was held at the end of the forty years in the wilderness to count the men of the next generation when all but two from the first census had died.[19] Those two men were Joshua and Caleb.

The second census introduced some more anomalies where for instance the numbers of Gad at 40,500 was the same as for Ephraim in the first census. Likewise, the numbers for Asher at 53,400 in the second census was the same as those of Naphtali in the first census. The same listings of numbers were either careless scribal errors, which is hard to accept from those devout masters or else it was downright extraordinary. Either way, it was another

---

[19] Book of Numbers Chapter 26

nail in the coffin for the notion of these sets of figures having been two censuses.

The trail had started with the quotes from the gospels at the birth of Jesus and involved several references to Ephraim, which had led to the scene with Jacob crossing his arms to bless his two grandsons. Jacob had broken with custom where he had blessed the younger grandson Ephraim with his right hand and here in the census, I now observed another anomaly. This was where Ephraim again stood out because he appeared before his older brother Manasseh in the first census. Jacob had forecast that Ephraim would be greater than Manasseh and this was true where the numbers for the younger son totaled 40,500 men as compared to 32,200 men for the older brother Manasseh.

I moved on to look at the second census of the tribes, which was held at the end of the forty years in the wilderness when all but two men from the first census had died. I found that Manasseh had regained his rightful place and appeared before Ephraim in this second census. This change of position seemed unimportant until I tried entering the numbers of both censuses onto a spreadsheet. It was an eye opener because the names and numbers for Ephraim and Manasseh formed a crossover as follows:

	1st census		2nd Census	
Ephraim	40,500		Manasseh	52,700
		✗		
Manasseh	32,200		Ephraim	32,500

The changeover of the names and numbers with both men formed into a crossover so the sign of a cross had again surfaced. Rather than go into too much numerical detail at this stage it is essential to let the cat out of the bag by performing computations, which were gleaned from the biblical instructions. When the numbers of Ephraim were added together and then halved the result was as follows:

40,500 + 32,500 = 73,000 ÷ 2 = 36,500

The sign of the cross had led into a maze behind the computations to reveal a very high visibility number where the average for Ephraim's two censuses came to 36,500. This number was the equivalent of one hundred solar years in whole days.

By following the clues from the prophets, the trail had led to the two censuses of the tribes of Israel to reveal a result which as Isaiah had stated **"that it be not a people."** The reference by Isaiah relating to 65 years was loaded for it pointed to Enoch whose first age was 65 years. But Enoch's final age was given at 365 years and here was that number multiplied by one hundred in the display for Ephraim as 36,500. Isaiah had stated **"that it be not a people"** and finding the number 36,500 with Ephraim and the earlier number of 35,400 with Benjamin suggested that instead those numbers were the days of a solar calendar.

There was also another reference and it was by Hosea, which further qualified the findings where the prophet referred to Ephraim stating **"The iniquity of Ephraim is bound up; his sin is hid."** [20] The prophet had specifically named Ephraim and as outlined, the solar related time of 36,500 with Ephraim was bound up and well hidden. Rachel had pointed the way like a signpost where the numbers of her son Benjamin and her grandson Ephraim represented the moon and sun respectively in the two data banks, which had been paraded as two censuses.

The potential of having two time periods prompted me to do some analysis on the other figures on the spreadsheet. I added

---

[20] Book of Hosea Chapter 13:12

up the numbers of Jacob's first wife Leah's sons in the first census. Their totals came to 292,200. As a time period the number converted to eight hundred solar years. The base period of 2,922 days or eight years was very important in astronomy and it is known as the Octaeteris. Again, the period looked to have been multiplied by one hundred. It was an encouraging next step in the quest and soon another oddity caught my attention where there was something unusual about the arrangements of Leah's five sons. In their midst were the numbers of Gad even though he was born to a different mother.

I then found that by adding on the numbers of Gad to Leah's five son's numbers the new total introduced the corrective synchronizing factor between the solar calendar year of 365.25 days and the actual solar year of 365.242 days. Without boring you with the mathematics it was suffice to say that this was a remarkable finding because that degree of clarity with solar time was thousands of years before its time. For instance, the Julian calendar dating from 45 BCE had a 365 ¼ day solar calendar and it went ten days out of tune before it was corrected by the Gregorian calendar in the 16th century CE to reflect the true solar year of 365.242 days. Was this finding just a fluke coincidence or did the ancients know precisely the true length of the solar year?

The numbers of the two censuses of the tribes of Israel were entered onto a spreadsheet. Then I added the numbers of each tribe in the first and second census together and then halved the totals to get the average number for each tribe. Because the initial analysis had shown that these were not the numbers of twelve tribes, I retitled them as the 1st chart and 2nd chart. The total of the numbers in both charts was entitled the 3rd chart and the average of the numbers was entitled the 4th chart. The analysis so far had indicated that the numbers were the days of a solar calendar and so that is why I listed the four charts in Table I as the days of a solar calendar. It was necessary to list the tribal names twice in the table because of the crossover between Ephraim and Manasseh as was outlined earlier.

Table 1: The Days of a Solar Calendar

Names in 1st Count	1st Chart Numbers		Names in 2nd Count	2nd Chart Numbers	3rd Chart Numbers	4th Chart Numbers
Reuben	46,500		Reuben	43,730	90,230	45,115
Simeon	59,300		Simeon	22,200	81,500	40,750
Gad	45,650		Gad	40,500	86,150	43,075
Judah	74,600		Judah	76,500	151,100	75,550
Issachar	54,400		Issachar	64,300	118,700	59,350
Zebulun	57,400		Zebulun	60,500	117,900	58,950
Ephraim	40,500	✗	Manasseh	52,700	84,900	42,450
Mannaseh	32,200		Ephraim	32,500	73,000	36,500
Benjamin	35,400		Benjamin	45,600	81,000	40,500
Dan	62,700		Dan	64,400	127,100	63,550
Asher	41,500		Asher	53,400	94,900	47,450
Naphtali	53,400		Naphtali	45,400	98,800	49,400
Total	603,550		Total	601,730		602,640

At that stage it was necessary to update the terminology in order to avoid confusion between references to censuses of men and calendar days. Therefore, the first and second censuses were retitled the first and second calendar charts. The totals of the numbers from those two charts were labelled the third calendar chart. In turn, the average of the totals from the third chart was labelled the fourth calendar chart. Because we are dealing with ancient arithmetic it is essential to state that numerical data was very different in antiquity but don't worry for, I have presented the finding using our contemporary numerical symbols and mathematical methods and it does not affect the validity of the numbers.[21]

This fourth calendar chart was where the majority of the calendar indices were archived so take a while and study how it was so cleverly hidden from public view. In effect it was a secret chamber where an archive of precious information was stored hidden behind those simple computations. So perfect was the method of concealment that it escaped the prying eyes of millions for almost three thousand years.

The scribes gave each segment the name of a tribe, which in turn was named after the ten sons and two grandsons of the patriarch Jacob. Thus, we had twelve groupings. There was more to follow because Jacob had in fact twelve sons and these were born to four different mothers. His first wife Leah had six sons while his second wife Rachel had two sons. There were also two hand maidens who were Zilpah and Bilah and they had two sons each by Jacob. Leah's son Levi and Rachel's son Joseph did not feature in the future twelve tribes. Instead, Joseph's two sons Ephraim and Manasseh took the places of Joseph and Levi. Thus, there were twelve mini groupings with the twelve men's names and four extra larger groupings with the four mother's names. To make things easier it is intended to stick to those names of the men and mothers during the forthcoming analysis. An outline of the all-important forth calendar chart is shown below in Table 2.

---

[21] For an understanding of ancient mathematics reference Neugebauer, O. *The Exact Sciences in Antiquity*, New York, Dover 1969 and also McLeish, John, Number: London: Bloomsbury, 1991.

Table 2: The Days of a Strategic Solar Calendar in the Fourth Chart

Leah	Leah	Zilpah	Leah	Leah	Leah	Rachel	Rachel	Rachel	Bilah	Zilpah	Bilah
Reuben	Simeon	Gad	Judah	Issachar	Zubulan	Manasseh	Ephraim	Benjamin	Dan	Asher	Napthali
45,115	40,750	43,075	75,550	59,350	58,950	42,450	36,500	40,500	63,550	47,450	49,400

Total of first seven numbers = 365,240 Days

    While conducting further analysis I added up the numbers of the tribes in the fourth chart one by one beginning with Reuben, then Simeon, then Gad, Judah, Issachar, Zebulun and then Manasseh. I was watching the calculator and saw the total after adding Manasseh came to 365,240 as shown in the table above. It was the equivalent of one thousand solar years to within two days. To achieve the exact target of one thousand years two more men would have been required relative to the census format. And lo and behold two men, Joshua and Caleb, had survived to be two extra in addition to the second census. This made the total complete at 365,242 for the number of days in one thousand solar years. It was the evidence I had been looking for where it showed that the biblical astronomer knew the true length of the solar year. There now was firm evidence from the analysis to indicate that the numbers, which were paraded as two censuses were instead the days of a solar calendar.

The Solar and Sidereal Years

    In the analysis it became evident that the biblical astronomers had applied the solar and sidereal years in some equations. These are technical terms that may be puzzling to the lay person and therefore, it is necessary to outline how there are two ways to measure the period of one year. The first is where the solar year is measured by reference to a fixed point on earth and it is 365.242 days long. We have seen that the biblical calendar above had recorded that precise period over the time of one thousand years or 365,240 days plus the extra two days with Joshua and Caleb.

The second way to measure the period of one year is where a bright star is used as the fixed point and this is called a star or sidereal year. The sidereal year is 365.256 days long and this is 20 minutes approximately longer than the solar year. In some of the analysis computations will involve both the solar year and the sidereal year.

Chapter 3

The Incredible Old Ages were in fact Time Periods

During the analysis I converted the numbers in each of the twelve segments in Chart 1 and Chart 2 of Table 1 above from days to solar years by dividing them by 365.242 in order to see if anything unusual would materialize. It seemed to me that some of the converted periods compared to those bizarre final ages of the patriarchs. For instance, the number of Ephraim at 40,500 in the first chart came to 110 years 321 days. This period equated to the final age of Ephraim's father Joseph who supposedly died at 110 years of age. A second example was with the conversion of the numbers of Naphtali at 53,400 in the 1st chart where the result was 146 years and 74 days. This period compared to Joseph's father Jacob who allegedly died when he was 147 years old. He may have been 146 years 74 days but it would be referred to as his 147th year.

It transpired that there were ten of the twenty four original segments in the 1st and 2nd charts whose converted numbers equated to the final age of Sarah and nine of the patriarchs. The ages of four of the patriarchs were also evident in the 4th chart. The comparisons with the ages are shown in Table 3.[22] Another cat was out of the bag and it

---

[22] The ages were obtained from the Bible or from the biblical Book of Jasher

Chapter 3 - The Incredible Old Ages were in fact Time Periods

revealed the true purpose of those incredible ages of the patriarchs – they were long periods in years.

Table 3: The Incredible Ages compare to the Converted periods of the Calendar

Names	Final Age	Names	Period in Years: 1st Chart
Sarah	127 years old	Reuben	127 years 114 days
Gad	125 years old	Gad	124 years 360 days
Joseph	110 years old	Ephraim	110 years 323 days
Zebulun	114 years old	Asher	113 years 227 days
Jacob	147 years old	Naphtali	146 years 74 days
			Period in Years: 2nd Chart
Moses	120 years old	Reuben	119 years 266 days
Reuben	125 years old	Benjamin	124 years 309 days
Joshua	110 years old	Gad	110 years 323 days
Judah	119 years old	Reuben	119 years 266 days
Simeon	120 years old	Reuben	119 years 266 days
			Period in Years: 4th Chart
Aaron	123 years old	Reuben	123 years 190 days
Jacob	130 years when in Egypt	Asher	129 years 333 days
Ishmael	137 years old	Naphtali	135 years 92 days
Abraham	175 years old	Dan	173 years 363 days

- Jacob was in the limelight where he appeared three times in the table. The first and second appearance was where his final age of 147 years compared to the converted numbers with Naphtali and Asher at 146 years 74 days in the 1st and 2nd charts respectively. However, there was another very important age in the life of Jacob where it stated very explicitly in scripture that he was 130 years old when he went to live in Egypt. This age of 130 years compared to the converted period of Asher in the fourth chart at 129 years 333 days.

- The final age of Judah was given in scripture as both 119 years and also 129 years. I have shown the 119 years comparison with Reuben in the table above. However, the 129 years also compared with the converted period of Asher in the 4th chart.

- The final age of Abraham at 175 years compared to the converted period with Dan which was two days short of 174 years. However, if Abraham had just turned 174 years to the day it would have been his 175th year. This was a difference of just two days. There was a solution to bridge the gap with those two days and it simply was to convert the period of 173 years 363 days from solar time to sidereal time and the result was 174 years to the very day. This conversion from solar time to sidereal time will feature again as the analysis progresses.

- The comparison with the converted period with Naphtali at 135 years 92 days was with Ishmael who died when he was 137 years old. If Ishmael died on his 136th birthday it would have been his 137th year. The difference between 135 years and 92 days with Asher and the final ages of Ishmael was exactly nine months. It seems that the biblical writers had included the nine months period of pregnancy to calculate the final age of Ishmael.

This outcome with Ismael was rather dramatic for it was the first biblical example to show that the nine months period of pregnancy could be included in the overall lifespan of a person. There was a second example where the difference between the final age of Jacob at 147 years and those of Naphtali in the first chart, was just two week longer than nine months. With two examples out of four names it seemed that the biblical scribes had indicated that life began at conception.

There was a second appearance of Jacob in the analysis and it was the age of 130 years when he moved to live in Egypt. This age of 130 years was used as a reference point to date events in Egypt from then on and this was outlined in the Book of Jasher. The same dating system was used during the reign of a king where for instance, it stated that it was in the fourth year of King Solomon's reign when he started to build the temple. However, with Jacob it was more than just in his own lifetime because the focal point of his move to Egypt continued on after his death making the reference the dating system of a calendar.

Those incredible ages have proved to be the public face of what lay hidden behind some of the numbers of the tribes and it was only when the figures were converted to solar years that their true purpose as long time periods of a solar calendar was revealed.

Chapter 4

Reconstructing the Biblical calendar

The exodus through the wilderness was the setting where the numbers of the secret records of astronomy were catalogued in disguise as mere domestic related indices. It was like uncovering an archaeological site and having to labor intensely to scrape away the sands of time in order to find out what lay beneath the surface. It was heavy going so bear with me for it will take time and effort to explain the numerical jewels, which were loaded with intelligent data. The first application with the solar calendar was to use the 4th chart to map out biblical history. This 4th chart spread out over a period of 1,650 years and already the period of one thousand years or 365,240 days had been revealed from the total of the numbers from Rueben down to Manasseh. Therefore, it was necessary to see if a corresponding period of one thousand years was evident in the biblical historical time line.

One possibility seemed to be from when King David died and Solomon became king down through the centuries to end at Jesus. For this period to fit the bill the scribes would have had to lay down an anchor point in the Bible so that future generations could identify the year when the one thousand years began or ended. I recalled there was such an anchor point in the gospels and on looking up the details I found it was in Luke's gospel where it referred to when John the Baptist began to preach as follows:

Chapter 4 - Reconstructing the Biblical calendar

"Now in the fifteenth year of the reign of Tiberius Caesar, Pontius Pilate being governor of Judea, and Herod being Tetrarch of Galilee and his brother Philip tetrarch of Ituraea and of the region of Trachonitis and Lysanias the tetrarch of Abilene." (Luke 3:1)

The gospel writer was certainly intent on identifying the year where he had listed so many important leaders beginning with Tiberius in the 15th year of his reign.

It is reckoned by historians that the 15th year of Tiberius was the year 29 CE. Jesus was six months younger than John and Luke tells us that his ministry began when he was about thirty years of age. The age of Jesus when he began to preach will be discussed in a later chapter. By applying the Roman dynastic reckoning for calculating the 15th year of Tiberius and adding on the extra six months for Jesus, it would bring us to the year 30 CE. That was the year when Jesus began to preach. By applying the one thousand year period from the anchor year of 30 CE the period led back to 970 BCE. (It should be noted that the conventional calendar had no year zero for it started in the year 1 CE and dated back in time from 1 BCE. Therefore, I have used the astronomical method of dating which allows for having a year zero.) It was a remarkable fit because it is reckoned that Solomon became king around that year.[23]

The next step in using the solar calendar was to map out the period from Solomon back to the exodus out of Egypt. This will involve the two different periods, which related to the time the Israelites spent in Egypt and also to the 480 years from the exodus to when Solomon started to build the temple, which was listed as in the fourth year of his reign. It outlined in the Book of Exodus that the Israelites spent 430 years in Egypt to

---

[23] It is a demanding task to try and date events in the Bible to the exact year so an error of one or two years or even more has to be accommodated.

the self-same day.[24] However, it outlined in the Book of Jasher that the time spent in Egypt was the period of 210 years.[25] These three different references concerning the exodus with the 430, 480 and 210 years have frustrated the biblical fraternity for no satisfactory theory had previously emerged to resolve the puzzle. A fourth period of 400 years relative to the sojourn in Egypt was cited by God to Abraham, but this interval had not raised as much interest.

The calendar period with the 4th chart had mapped out the period of 1,000 years of 365,240 days from the thirty year old Jesus in 30 CE to when Solomon became king in 970 BCE. This period of 1,000 years was the total of the first seven numbers from Reuben onto Manasseh in the 4th chart of the solar calendar. Thereafter, there were five segments of the calendar left with the numbers of Ephraim, Benjamin, Dan, Asher and Naphtali. I did the sums and found that the addition of the numbers of Ephraim and Benjamin came to 77,000 days. In turn, this period converted to 210 years 299 days. It was an eye opener because it compared favorably to the 210 years the Israelites spent in Egypt as was outlined in the Book of Jasher.

I then found that the combined numbers of Ephraim, Benjamin, Asher and Naphtali came to 476 years with only five days of a shortfall. Now both eyes were open because the period of 476 years was the time given from the exodus out of Egypt to when Solomon became king. I.e., Solomon started to build the temple in the fourth year of his reign, which was 480 years after the exodus. (480 – 4 = 476 years)

It was an amazing revelation for the two periods of 210 years and 476 years were included in the last five segments of the calendars 4th chart. However, there was a problem where the four names and numbers of Ephraim, Benjamin, Asher and Naphtali should have been in sequence from Solomon in 970 BCE back to the exodus. However, I found that the biblical

---

[24] Book of Exodus Chapter 12:41.
[25] Book of Jasher 81:3.

writers had left "*a fix*" to resolve the problem and it related to those incredible ages of the patriarchs.

Reorganising the last Five Names and Numbers in the 4th Chart

Because the ages of the patriarchs matched up with some of the periods in the time-charts it introduced a novel possibility. It afforded the opportunity to swivel the names in the 4th chart around to achieve a new alignment based on the natural genealogy of the patriarchs. The names and numbers which made up the calendar time-charts obviously needed to be positioned in the original alignments for the creators to produce so many of those magnificent time periods relative to the heavenly orbits as will be shown in a later chapter. In doing so, the designers gradually backed themselves into a corner where the overall final configuration could not be achieved without some very creative maneuverings. They did just that and majestically achieved a whole new realm of possibilities where they introduced the interexchange of the names and numbers. The designers had given a demonstration upfront of this interchanging where they had swapped over the numbers of 40,500 with Ephraim in the 1st chart with Gad in the 2nd chart. They did likewise with 53,400 with the numbers of Naphtali in the 1st chart with Asher in the 2nd chart.

This new re-alignment in the 4th chart allowed for an entry path for Abraham, Ishmael and Jacob to be introduced into the equation in seniority format. In this regard the original patriarchs stood like godfathers or sponsors for their appointed god-child in the order of their generations as is shown in Diagram 1. This role of sponsors had been indicated by Jacob where he crossed his arms to place his right hand on Ephraim.[26] This caused

---

[26] Book of Genesis 48:8-19.

Ephraim to jump in seniority before his older brother Manasseh in the first census, but he was interchanged back into his natural place in the second census.

Diagram 1: The Sponsors stand over Five Tribes

Ephraim	Benjamin	Jacob	Ishmael	Abraham
Ephraim	Benjamin	Asher	Naphtali	Dan
99 years 341 days	110 years 323 days	129 years 333 days	135 years 92 days	173 years 363 days

In this realignment, the generations were instrumental in deciding the natural sequence of the names and associated numbers. I.e., Abraham was from the oldest generation so he came first and then came his son Ishmael and he was placed second and after him was Jacob in third place. Benjamin and Ephraim fell naturally into place because they were the next two generations. Isaac was the missing link in the chain of the original patriarchs for he died at 180 years of age. In his place instead was his half-brother Ishmael and it made it a full sequence in the order of the generations from Abraham down to Ephraim.

The names of Ephraim, Benjamin, Asher and Naphtali were now in sequence from Solomon being crowned king and the total of their time periods of 475 years 360 days dated back to the exodus out of Egypt. It was just five days short of 476 years. This appeared to be another example of where solar years were to be converted to sidereal years. The period of 475 solar years 360 days converted to 476 sidereal years 1 day. It was the second example of converting solar years to sidereal years for the first was with the conversion with the period of Dan at 173 solar years 363 days to 174 sidereal years to the very day. Those two examples were very important because they showed that sidereal years were part of the biblical writer's agenda with respect to the timing of the exodus.

The reconstructed part of the calendar is displayed in Diagram 2.

Chapter 4 - Reconstructing the Biblical calendar

Diagram 2: The Messiah Calendar Timeline in the 4th Chart

	Reuben	Simeon	Gad	Judah	Issachar	Zebulun	Manasseh	Ephraim	Benjamin	Asher	Naphtali	Dan	
A	Years	Years	Years	Years	Years	Years	Years	Years	Years	Years	Years	Years	
JESUS	123.52	111.57	117.93	206.85	162.5	161.4	116.22	99.93	110.88	129.91	135.25	173.99	
	↓												
B				365,240 Days or 1,000 Years		←―― 1,650 Years ――→			←― 476 Years ―→				
C	30 CE						970 BCE				1,446 BCE		1,620

The outline of the diagram is as follows:

A: The twelve calendar segments of the 4th chart as applied from the tribal names and their total numbers came to 1,650 solar years.

B: The total is broken down into the period of 1,000 years of 365,240 days from the first seven names in sequence. It led back from the thirty-year-old Jesus in 30 CE to when Solomon was crowned king in the year 970 BCE. This was immediately followed with the period of 476 years from the rearranged names and numbers of Ephraim, Benjamin, Asher and Naphtali. The period compared exactly from the exodus to when Solomon was crowned king as inferred in the first Book of Kings. It placed the exodus to the year 1,446 BCE.

C: The complete timeline from 30 CE back to 1,620 BCE with a year zero added in.

The total of the numbers for the twelve names in sequence added up to 1,650 years. This period was subdivided in order to highlight how the two periods of 1,000 and 476 years were structured into the 4th chart. To identify how the periods fitted into the biblical historical timeline it was necessary to start with Jesus where he began his ministry. I have already outlined about where it stated in Luke's gospel that John began to preach in the 15th year of the Roman emperor Tiberius. Tiberius became sole emperor after Augustus died on the 19th August 14 CE. Therefore, John began his ministry in the year 29 CE. Jesus was six months younger than John and it was reasonable to assume that his ministry began at the beginning of 30 CE. Because there were other timing

Chapter 4 - Reconstructing the Biblical calendar

factors in the overall configuration to be considered, I have applied the year 30 CE as the year that Jesus began his ministry.

Immediately following those seven names, which made up the 1,000 years, was the period of 476 years with the total of the numbers of Ephraim, Benjamin, Asher and Naphtali. This period was recognizable where in the first Book of Kings it stated that Solomon began to build the temple in the fourth year of his reign, which was quoted as 480 years after the Exodus.[27] He was therefore crowned king 476 years after the exodus out of Egypt.

---

[27] First Book of Kings Chapter 6:1.

Chapter 5

The Reed-777 Day Formula

Time passed by elusively in those ancient times while priests performed sacred ceremonies hoping to gain redemption with the Lord in the heavens. Days were counted and seasons blessed in sacred rituals with toil and denial, all sanctified by divine providence from the heavenly kingdom. Somewhere along the biblical highway the priests developed a method to master time and bring order into their nomadic lifestyles. This novel way probably started on an abacus. The priests developed a method of counting out the days in units of 777 days. This method was the key formula to resolve many of the biblical mysterious riddles relating to clusters of the number seven, which adorn the Bible. It was necessary to reveal this formula at this stage because it will impact later on the findings with a sacred timeline of the Messiah.

During the research work I conducted a simulation exercise in measuring time in lots of 777 days to see if it had a relationship with the solar year. It transpired that when 777 days was counted out and the exercise repeated for fifty five times, the measurement of time returned to practically the same anniversary date every 117 years. It only required the subtraction of two leap days to make the measurement exact to the very day. When the measurement was continued with the 777-day cycle, it returned to almost the same anniversary date after 217 years. Those circular motions with seven priests walking around the walls of

Chapter 5 - The Reed-777 Day Formula

Jericho blowing on seven ram's horns over seven days now made a lot more sense. It appeared to be a dress rehearsal to inform us to count out the days and measure time in intervals of seven days together with the imagery that seemed to suggest the bigger period of 777 days.

The three main numbers with this 777 day formula were thus 777, 117 and 217. I checked to see if there were any signs of these three numbers in the Bible and found that Methuselah's son Lamech lived to be 777 years of age. Ok it was not 777 days and you can be sure it was not 777 years because nobody ever lived to be that old. There were however more surprises in store for I deciphered how the scribes had encrypted those three numbers in the Old Testament. The first inkling of this encryption was with King Hezekiah where he made a burnt offering of seven bullocks, seven rams and seven lambs to the lord.[28] When I entered those animals and number onto a spreadsheet a strange mirage formed in front of my eyes. It was like when you go to get your eyes tested and the optician uses many different lenses to see how well you can read letters and numbers. On this exercise the numbers on the spreadsheet looked as follows:

Bullocks	Rams	Lambs
7	7	7

Without the words denoting animals, the three numbers looked like the bigger number of 777. But was this merging of the numbers to form the bigger number of 777 intended by the scribes or were my eyes playing tricks with me?

This was a burnt offering and I soon found that there were several more burnt offerings listed in the Old Testament and all had the same format of bullock, rams and lambs. One of those burnt offerings was in Chapter 29

---

[28] Second Book of Chronicles 29:21

of the Book of Numbers. In that chapter, Moses had made burnt offering, which were spread out over ten different days of the month. There were however three offerings among them, which had the same numbers of animals and they were with the sacrifice of one bullock, one ram and seven lambs. When those numbers were entered in tabular format onto a spreadsheet the visual content was quite apparent as follows:

Bullocks	Rams	Lambs
1	1	7

The merged numbers formed into the bigger number of **117** and that was another of the numbers on the search list.

The numerical trail was becoming predictable for one could not help but call in next door to Chapter 28 of the Book of Numbers where Moses also made burnt offerings to the Lord on three different feast days. One of the offerings was made on the fifteenth day of the month and it was the feast of the Passover. All three offerings comprised of two bullocks, one ram and seven lambs. These animal names proved to be notations. In tabular format those numbers merged into the bigger number as follows:

Bullocks	Rams	Lambs
2	1	7

Yes, it was the merged numbers of **217**. It had become all so easy for 217 was the second period which could be measured out in lots of 777 days to practically the same anniversary date with the solar year. There were only those two periods of 117 and 217 years, which gave those same anniversary outcomes. Longer term periods after that were multiples of 117 or 217 years or combinations thereof.

Chapter 5 - The Reed-777 Day Formula

Therefore, the portfolio with the three merged numbers of 777, 117 and 217 was complete. The greatest method of encryption ever devised had finally been deciphered.

The unit of 777 days proved to be the key to resolve many mysterious numerical riddles in the Bible. For instance, I soon discovered that the 777 day formula was also used to measure out the difference between solar and sidereal time. The difference was only twenty minutes and ten seconds and this tiny interval would have been impossible to measure before the advent of mechanical clocks. However, if the twenty minutes and ten seconds period was projected over a long time span, it added up to one day in every 72 years. The finding became more remarkable when I discovered that the difference added up to 1.67 days in 117 years. That was the same as the overlap in days when measuring time with the 777 day formula. I.e., $777 \times 55 = 42{,}735$ whereas 117 years = 42,733.33 days an overlap of 1.67 days.

I later discovered the hard evidence to show that the biblical mathematicians had projected the twenty minutes and ten second difference between sidereal and solar time over the period of 3,000 years. There were four such periods of 3,000 years and they added up to what was known as the Zoroastrian time of the long dominion of 12,000 years. Zoroaster was a Persian philosopher and during my biblical research work, I encountered several examples of his computations with the time of the long dominion encoded in scripture.

Finally, it was time to baptize this 777 day calendar system with a name. There were several references in the Bible to measuring with a reed. One of those references was in the Book of Revelation and the evidence suggested that the reed was a name of the 777 day method of measuring time.[29] Therefore, I have called this method of measuring time the Reed-777 day formula.

---

[29] Book of Revelation 11:1, 22:15, 16

Chapter 6

The Messiah Immortalised in Time

The biblical prophets predicted that a Messiah would come at the time of a star. His mission would be to prepare the straight path to salvation and open up the kingdom of heaven to the faithful. Christians believe that the prophecies were fulfilled and that Jesus was the Saviour. In contrast, the Jews do not accept that Jesus was the Messiah and they still await an anointed one. But now there was new evidence to show that the predictions were real because they were supported by a very detailed calendar planning process. This pre-planning overlaid a sacred timeline on the Bible and it ran from Abraham down to Jesus as was outlined earlier. The timeline included the life of Jesus from his birth at the time of an unusual star until his preaching career began and extended to the time of his crucifixion and resurrection.

What we know about Jesus is from the New Testament and it mainly relates to his teaching though it did give some personal details about his family. The gospels tell us he was born in Bethlehem at the time of a census and that three wise men came visiting the new born king because they had seen his star in the east. We know his mother was Mary and his stepfather was Joseph. After Jesus was born, the holy family had to escape to Egypt because the paranoid King Herod ordered the slaughter of all male children in order to eliminate a possible rival for his throne. It can be ascertained from references in the gospels that Jesus had brothers. When he was twelve years old, he went missing from his parents for three

Chapter 6 - The Messiah Immortalised in Time

days until they found him in the temple where he was astounding all the elders with his wisdom. Thereafter, the gospels were silent about Jesus until he began his preaching ministry at about thirty years of age.

It is generally taken that Jesus preached for three years. He chose twelve men from humble backgrounds to be his apostles. The stereo image of Jesus is of a very serious man who never seemed to smile but he had all the right answers despite the many challenges he encountered with the Pharisees and Sadducees. He was the devout holy man who preached of love and justice but yet he was not shy about denouncing '*holier than thou*' religious customs. If we look at Jesus through a different lens, we may be able to view how the prophets and gospel writers managed his image to make him a unique celebrity.

It began where there was no room at the Inn for Mary or Joseph and so the son of God was born in a stable and laid in a manger. It would bring tears to any eyes and such a humble beginning has possibly never since been equaled for the birth of a prodigy. Despite the humble surrounding, to be worshipped by three foreign dignitaries or Magi and proclaimed as a king had the prestige of casting a royal halo over the new born baby. But then there came the tension where the holy family had to flee to Egypt to escape from Herod's henchmen.

Solomon was renowned for his wisdom but compared to Jesus he never got beyond nursery school. Jesus seemed to know all the answers and he would have won a Nobel Prize for his words of divine inspiration. We were told in the gospels that Jesus performed many miracles where he turned water into wine, walked on water and raised Lazarus from the dead. These were paranormal feats and they may have astonished the followers in those days but those miracles were never subjected to the cold eye of scientific scrutiny. Jesus did cast a charismatic spell on the growing audiences and he seemed to have been a natural healer.

Because of his radical views Jesus was seen as a threat by the establishment who eventually had him arrested. To be betrayed by a friend for thirty pieces of silver was all the more harrowing seeing that it fitted in with the prophecies. Jesus was interrogated by the chief priests and also by the Roman Governor Pilate. He was scourged at a pillar and suffered the pain and ignominy of having a crown of thorns placed upon his head? This was followed by the most terrible torture of all where he was crucified. He was buried but on the third day his disciples found the tomb open and his body gone. He appeared first to Mary Magdalene and gave her the exalted role of telling the apostles about his resurrection. During the following forty days he magically appeared to the apostles before he ascended up to heaven. This was a powerful traumatic story with a very sadistic end and it won the hearts and minds of sympathizers throughout the centuries.

In my research I have read numerous books from the biblical and archaeological schools looking to learn more about the man himself but there was very little extra to tell. It was strange that such a remarkable man who lectured in the temple and elsewhere to the masses never wrote a note or letter himself which has ever came to light? He did write at the feet of the woman who was about to be stoned to death for adultery but that script was in the shifting sands of time. Because he had no personal belongings there was no legacy for him to bequeath and so there are no relics to venerate. The one remnant which followers hung onto was the shroud of Turin being his burial garb. Its authenticity however was dashed when scientific tests proved the fabric dated from the 13th century. Arising from particular anomalies in choosing the fabric sample, new tests are demanded but the Vatican ponders.

This is where an awkward void arises for there is no concrete evidence to prove Jesus was for real. If such a charismatic preacher had been tried by Pilate and later executed you would think there would have been some state records of the events. Even the contemporary

Chapter 6 - The Messiah Immortalised in Time

historians of his day never mention him albeit with one exception. There was a snippet by Josephus about Jesus but many academics have long since classified this entry as a later day forgery. If this investigation was a court of law the judge would issue a *habeas corpus*, which is literally a decree to produce the body. But this was always going to be a non-runner with Jesus.

It is against that background that we continue the investigation to see if extra evidence will emerge with respect to Jesus. No matter how sacred those prophecies were held to be by the faithful, they still were only words that were open to interpretation depending on the observer's point of view. All through this presentation I have stuck to numerical evidence to unveil an untold story, which was lying beneath the surface of scripture. This included the solar calendar to measure out the period of one thousand years from the thirty year old Jesus to when Solomon was crowned king. But thankfully there is more evidence in store and it will show that the prophets had plotted out the timeline and remarkably, it stopped at the year 33 CE, which is understood to be the year when Jesus was crucified.

For Jesus to be the predicted Messiah he would literally have had to be in the right place at the right time as laid out by the prophets. From those prophecies or forecasts you have just read it was reasonable to accept that Bethlehem would be the place where the Messiah would be born. That part of the prophecy could have been seen to be fulfilled by the gospel writers entering the place of birth as Bethlehem. The Messiah would be born at the time of an unusual star however was not as clear cut because there would have been so many sightings of bright stars in the centuries after the prophets had made their forecasts. Therefore, the forecast about a star was too vague. But now for the first time we have the records with the solar calendar to consult in order to see if they contained the indices that would identify the Star of Bethlehem.

The Star of Bethlehem

One of the popular theories for the identity of the Star of Bethlehem was that it may have been a triple conjunction of Jupiter and Saturn in the year 7 BCE. A triple conjunction is where the planets of Jupiter and Saturn come very close together three times over a six month period. The triple conjunction in 7 BCE was in the constellation of pieces and it is a spectacle, which happens every 794 years 146 days. Therefore, the previous conjunction with those planets of Jupiter and Saturn in the constellation of Pieces before 7 BCE would have been in the year 801 BCE approximately. By starting at a common starting date in 801 BCE there would have been 27 orbits of Saturn at 795 years 131 days to the year 7 and 6 BCE. There was also the period of 794 years 146 days with the triple conjunction itself. Thus, there were two possible parameters which the biblical astronomer may have applied to identify the Star of Bethlehem as Jupiter and Saturn coming close together. Those parameters were as follows:

Triple Conjunction every 794 years 146 days

Saturn by 27 orbits = 795 years 131 days

There was no technical data previously to verify the theory of the triple conjunction having been the Star of Bethlehem but now there was the solar calendar to consult. It would have required a computer program to check the number combination of the solar calendar for a total of 794 years 146 days and 795 years 131 days but thankfully the gospel writers had done the job for us. This was where I noticed that the names of six tribal leaders with Judah, Simeon, Asher, Ephraim, Naphtali and Zebulun were listed in the gospels but mainly at the birth of birth of Jesus. Because of the statement about Rachel weeping for her children it was obvious that her son Benjamin, who was also born in Bethlehem, was insinuated in the gospels.

I added up the numbers of those named leaders and found that six of their calendar segments in the 2nd chart had a total as follows:

Simeon + Judah + Zebulun + Ephraim + Asher + Naphtali = 795 years 132 days

This result compared to 795 years 131 days for 27 orbits of Saturn, which occurred between the triple conjunction in 801 BCE and its repeat performance in the year 7 BCE.

This was an astonishing result but it was only achieved with the name dropping hints from the gospel writers. Despite the uniqueness of the result sceptics would say that it was just an amazing coincidence. Therefore, the biblical testimony of two witnesses was required to place the findings on a firm footing. The next result was in the 4th chart and it was as follows:

Simeon + Judah + Benjamin + Ephraim + Asher + Naphtali = 794 years 147 days

This second result compared to 794 years 146 days between the triple conjunction in 801 BCE and the triple conjunction in 7 BCE. It was the second witness to identify the Star of Bethlehem as a triple conjunction of Jupiter and Saturn.

With breath-taking precision two important parameters from the triple conjunction of Jupiter and Saturn every 794.4 years had matched up with six of the seven tribal names of Simeon, Judah, Ephraim, Asher Naphtali, Benjamin and Zebulun. One group was in the 2nd chart while the other was in the 4th chart. All that it required was to exchange Benjamin with Zebulun in both charts to create two of the recognizable periods relative to forming the multiple orbits that identified with a triple conjunction of Jupiter and Saturn. The identity of the Star over Bethlehem was now on a scientific footing because the orbital details were to hand to verify it was that triple conjunction.

Date of Birth of Jesus

Having identified the Star of Bethlehem I set about examining if the timing aspects with the triple conjunction fitted in with the periods, which were quoted in the gospels surrounding the conception and birth of John and Jesus. Astronomers have calculated that the first phase of the triple conjunction occurred where the two planets came very close to each other on the 27th May of 7 BCE in the constellation of pieces. The two planets then parted but they came back close together on the 6th October 7 BCE. They again parted company but returned almost together on the 1st December 7 BCE. The two planets then went their own way and that ended the triple conjunction. But there was still a rare spectacle in sight where there was what Hughes called a *'fiery triangle'* of Jupiter, Saturn and Mars around the 26th February 6 BCE on the border of Pieces and Aries.[30] Therefore, there were precise dates with the conjunctions of Jupiter and Saturn and the fiery triangle of Jupiter, Saturn and Mars to try and match up with the timing of the events in the gospels.

We were told in the gospels that an angel called Gabriel visited an old priest named Zachary and foretold that his aged wife Elizabeth would bear a son. Elizabeth got pregnant and for some peculiar reason she hid herself away for five month. Thereafter, we were told that the

---

[30] Astronomical Thoughts on the Star of Bethlehem by David W Hughes, P128-130 at https://books.google.ie/books?isbn=9004308474

Chapter 6 - The Messiah Immortalised in Time

angel Gabriel visited Mary and she miraculously got pregnant from '*on high.*' Mary then visited Elizabeth and it was in the 6th month of her cousin's pregnancy. Elizabeth's baby jumped in her womb when the two women met. This was a similar occurrence to what had happened to Rebecca centuries beforehand when the twins Esau and Jacob had stirred in her womb.[31] Mary stayed with Elizabeth for around three months and that was about the time when John would have been born. Meanwhile the Magi were on their way following a peculiar star.

Now let us match up those time periods in the gospels with those in the triple conjunction in 7 BCE and the fiery triangle of the planets in February 6 BCE. Hughes pointed out that during late 8 BCE and early 7 BCE the planets of Jupiter and Saturn approached each other. For reasons that you will soon see, I have taken December in the year 8 BCE to be the starting date of when Elizabeth got pregnant with her son John. She then hid away for five months, which brought the proceedings up to late April or the beginning of May in 7 BCE. What was so special about the five months in hiding by Elizabeth and was the period reflected in the triple conjunction? I found a reference that the movements of Jupiter and Saturn would have started to become noticeable in late April of 7 BCE because the two planets had come to within three degrees of each other and this was a limit, which would have applied over the course of the next eight months.[32] Therefore, there was a possible correlation with Elizabeth hiding for five months and the lead in to the triple conjunction with Jupiter and Saturn from late in 8 BCE to late April in 7 BCE.

The gospels tell us that Mary was visited by the Angel Gabriel. Let us imagine that the visit took place on the 27th May 7 BCE, which was when the first occurrence

---

[31] Book of Genesis 25:22, 23
[32] Reference www.space.com

of the triple conjunction took place. Mary then visited Elizabeth and it stated that it was in the sixth month of her cousin's pregnancy. Mary stayed with Elizabeth for around three months, which would bring the proceedings up to sometime around the 27th August in 7 BCE. That would have also been the time when John was born. There was six months to go with Mary's pregnancy and that would have brought the events right up to the 26th February in 6 BCE. The period from the 27th May 7 BCE to the 26th February in 6 BCE was exactly nine months or the same as Mary's pregnancy.

By applying those dates and time periods we could deduct that Jesus was born on the 26th of February in the year 6 BCE. That is what the findings suggest for the whole event with Mary's pregnancy and the associated time periods in the gospels were a reflection of the heavens beginning with the conception of Jesus at the first phase of the conjunction of Jupiter and Saturn on the 27th day of May in 7 BCE. It ended with the fiery triangle of Jupiter, Saturn and Mars together on February 26th in 6 BCE. A layout of the timing events with the dates of the conception and births of John and Jesus is shown on Diagram 3 below.

Chapter 6 - The Messiah Immortalised in Time

Diagram 3: The Conception and Births of John and Jesus

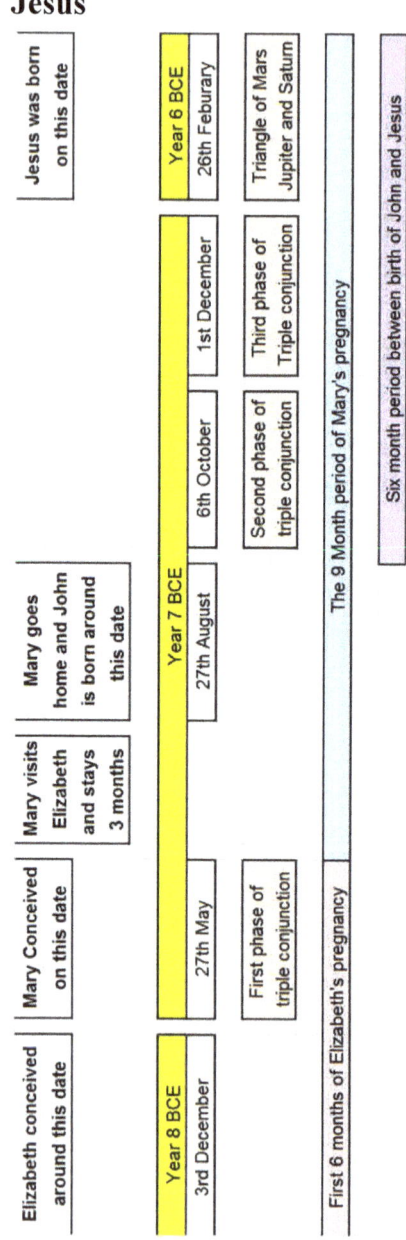

The prime dates were plotted against the first phase of the triple conjunction on the 27th May in 7 BCE when we could assume that was when Jesus may have been conceived. It continued to the spectacle with Jupiter, Saturn and Mars on the 26th February in 6 BCE when he was possibly born. It was a nine month period exactly and it was the deciding factor in selecting those two dates.

I have listed the conception of John as the 3rd December in the year 8 BCE. It was always going to be around that date but there was one final cosmic aspect to possibly adjudicate on the issue. The time period from the 3rd December in 8 BCE to the 26th February in 6 BCE added up to 450 days. This total was two orbits of the planet Venus. I traced back from the date of the birth of Jesus by applying two orbits of Venus. This led back to the 3rd December in 8 BCE and so that date was applied for the time of John's conception.

That exercise was like placing the various pieces of a jigsaw into their respective places. But now it is time to cast a critical eye on the whole proceedings. A prophet named Balaam had foretold that: *"there shall come a Star out of Jacob, and a Sceptre shall rise out of Israel."* (Numbers 24:17) The quote did refer to a star and a sceptre indicates somebody with royal power or authority. This prophecy was used by the court advisors of Herod to tell the king why the Magi were enquiring about a new born king because they had seen his star. Thus, the star at Bethlehem was seen by the gospel writers to fulfill the prophecy by Balaam. In turn, the gospel writers had factored in those tribal names, which made it easy to identify those two parameters of a triple conjunction in the solar calendar.

The details so far were normal enough and the gospel writers appeared to have just recorded the facts as they saw them. Even the Magi enquiring about a new born king because they had seen his star could be explained away as they expected input from astrologers. But now there comes the paranormal element for it would be truly unbelievable if a child prodigy happened to be born at the time of that triple conjunction. Yet the gospel writers included the five months, three months and the implied last six months, which linked Jesus to that star.

That concludes the investigation on the star of Bethlehem and so the analysis can move on to identify the complete stretch of the Messiah timeline and the various methods that were applied to lay out that lengthy period. We have seen in an earlier chapter that the biblical calendar measured the period from the thirty year old Jesus in 30 CE back to Solomon and onto the date of the exodus and then onto the year 1,620 BCE. There was a second method which ran in parallel with the solar calendar and it was with the periods in years of the Reed-777 day formula.

777 Days by 777 Times

I discovered that a timeline of 777 days by 777 times was superimposed on the historical events of the Bible and it ran in parallel with the solar calendar. The 777 days by 777 times timeline was derived from the Reed-777 day formula. Its constituent elements were those three periods of 117 years and the three periods of 217 years, which were decoded from Chapters 28 and Chapter 29 of the Book of Numbers. This must rank as the greatest method of encryption ever devised because it escaped the prying eyes of every generation for nearly three thousand years. It required applying the three periods of 117 years but twice the three periods of 217 years to form the complete time line. To trace how the virtual time line was superimposed on biblical history it was necessary to home in on the era when the Torah was re-edited and that included the time of King Josiah.

The biblical writers were quite vociferous about the exemplary character of King Josiah and openly declared that not since Moses had there been such a righteous leader. They also credited him with holding a huge Passover feast the likes of which had not been seen since the time of Samuel. There was no doubt but that Josiah was the darling of the biblical writers especially as he brought in new religious reforms and centralized the burnt offering sacrifices at the temple. His great grandfather King Hezekiah had originally introduced similar reforms of centralized worship at the temple but these had fallen by the wayside during the long reign of his son Manasseh.

While reading the history of Hezekiah, his son Manasseh, his grandson Amon and finally Josiah, I noticed that the years in which they reigned were listed. I did the mental arithmetic and the result revealed a startling total as follows:

Hezekiah	Manasseh	Amon	Josiah	
29 +	55 +	2 +	31	= 117 years

The four periods added up to 117 years and this was one of the periods of the Reed-777-day formula. It seemed to be an example of how to date the events with the four kings in the Bible and it used the period of 117 years as the template. The solar calendar had an anchor date where it began on the 15th year of the reign of Tiberius and likewise, the Reed-777-day periods had also to be anchored in time. Because the reed period of 117 years stood out like a sample prototype to measure biblical history I took it to be the era when the anchor point was set by the biblical writers. But it would need a particular year to set the starting date.

While trying to identify a possible starting date I came across a very unusual matter with Josiah, which aroused my attention. Josiah was named in a prediction by a prophet called Shemaiah over three hundred years before the king was born. Shemaiah was known as a man from God and he stood fast against King Jeroboam who had made two golden calves and also made sacrilegious offerings in the high places of Bethel and Dan. The man of God vented his anger at such idolatrous profanities when he confronted Jeroboam at the altar in Bethel. The prophecy was outlined in the first Book of Kings as follows:

"O altar, altar, thus saith the Lord; Behold, a child shall be born to the house of David. Josiah by name; and upon thee shall he offer the priests of the high places that burn incense upon thee, and men's bones shall be burnt upon thee."[33]

It must stand out as the most clear-cut prophecy in the whole Bible because it actually named the future king, Josiah. There was more to follow where King Jeroboam stretched out his hand pointing at the man of God and said *'lay hold on him.'* But the king's hand shrivelled up with the fingers outstretched. The finger was left pointing at the man of God and it was the words he said, which were in the limelight.

Centuries later where there was a royal descendant of David named Josiah. The finger pointing exercise had thus bore fruit and it led to the 18th year of Josiah for that was when something unusual occurred. The high priest Hilkiah found a sacred book during restoration work at Solomon's temple and the book was attributed to Moses. Josiah became enraged when the book was read to him and he carried out the words of the prophecy by the man of God. He destroyed the high places of idolatrous worship and burnt the bones of the priests who were buried at Bethel.

Because it was referred to as the book of the Law of Moses the common theory was that the book that was

---

[33] First Book of Kings Chapter 13:2

found in the temple was possibly the Book of Deuteronomy. But this recent discovery with the revelation on the true purpose of those numbers in the Bible sheds a completely new light on its identity. It has been well established by academics that the Torah or first five books of the Old Testament were covertly re-edited around the time of Josiah. The revision changed the whole complexion of the Torah where it introduced new stringent laws of religious worship, which included centralization of sacrificial rituals. This could be explained as the priests opening up their private holy ceremonial scrolls to the public by writing the details into scripture. The revisionism included the addition of some very strange material where it comprised of practically the whole Book of Numbers. Those numbers included the two alleged censuses, which were shown earlier as the days of a solar calendar. More of those inserted numbers were in the burnt offerings that were at the heart of the reed formula.

All the re-editing was done in secret and the numbers were disguised as domestic book keeping issues obviously to hide their true identity and purpose. It would now appear that the long lost book that was found in the temple was instead the new revised Torah. It seems as if the revisionists organized a book launch and they had fingered Josiah to be the PR spokesman. In other words, the revisionists pretended the revised Torah was the actual original book, which was supposedly written by Moses many centuries beforehand. The most important issue for this investigation however was the date when the book launch took place. Scholars date the finding of the book to the year 622 BCE but some historians dispute this date. Therefore, it was necessary to try and see if this new series of discoveries could shed a new light on the actual year.

Some scholars are of the opinion that Josiah was born in 648 BCE. He was eight years old when he ascended the throne and so his 18th year would have been

Chapter 6 - The Messiah Immortalised in Time

in the year 622 BCE. The king reigned for thirty one years and therefore he would have died in 609 BCE. But the year of his death is challenged by some historians who argue that it was more likely to have been in the year 606 BCE relative to the king's participation in a specific battle. We have seen how the biblical astronomers had factored in the indices to identify a triple conjunction of Jupiter and Saturn in the year 7 BCE. That anchor point in the heavens prompted me to check and see if the biblical astronomers had also aligned the 18th year of Josiah with a celestial sign.

I found that there was an unusual phenomenon in what is called a transit of Mercury across the face of the sun around that time. When Mercury crosses the face of the sun it causes a tiny eclipse and it happened in October of 618 BCE. On checking further, I found that there was also a transit of Mercury in 644 BCE and another transit in 605 BCE. Transits of Mercury occur in fairly regular periods of 13, 33 and 217 years and there will be a detailed discussion on them later in the book.

The amazing aspect about those three transits was that the difference in time between their three periods mirrored the same periods with the ages of Josiah. To display this comparison more clearly let's say that Josiah was born in the same year as the transit of Mercury in 644 BCE. He was eight years old when he began to reign and therefore his 18th year would have been in 618 BCE and his death in 605 BCE. These dates were arrived at using astronomical years, which are one year less than dates given in BCE and this is because there was no year zero between BCE and CE. It meant that the astronomical year of 605 BCE was the same as the biblical year of 606 BCE and that was the same year that some historians identify as the year of the death of Josiah.

The evidence with the transits of Mercury mirroring the ages of Josiah was exceptional. To have one comparison would be coincidence, to have two would be enough to ask awkward questions but to have three in biblical terms was conclusive. It indicated that the cosmic configuration had been the determining factor with the biblical astronomers in deciding the year of launching what was deemed to be a lost book of Moses. They thus possibly chose the transit of Mercury in the year 618 BCE as the pivotal point to anchor the Reed-777 day periods in order to map out a sacred timeline. This would resolve the debated position about the actual year of the death of Josiah for it showed his ages to be part of the virtual timeline of the Messiah in the heavens above. The dating process of overlaying the Reed-777 day periods of 117 and 217 years could thus begin and the starting year was on 18th year of the reign of Josiah and the date was decided by the transit of Mercury on the 11th October 618 BCE.

There were three periods of 117 years, which had earlier been decoded from Chapter 29 of the Book of Numbers. Because Josiah had been named back in the time Jeroboam, I decided to date events back in time from Josiah. The three periods of 117 years led back to the year 969 BCE. (970 BCE with biblical dating) It was a sensational result for it is reckoned by historians to be the possible time that King David died and his son Solomon was crowned king. Importantly, it also was in the twelve month period with the one thousand years from Jesus in 30 CE back to Solomon in the year 970 BCE as was outlined with the solar calendar. When dating biblical events, a target to within a twelve month period is understandable because the Bible does not always quote the month of an event.

The three periods of 117 years were all utilized back to Solomon but there were still the three periods of 217 years from the merged numbers in Chapter 29 of the Book of Numbers to be applied. Historical events are very sketchy before Solomon but I added the three periods of

Chapter 6 - The Messiah Immortalised in Time

217 years to 969 BCE and it led to 1,620 BCE. The building blocks of the jigsaw were falling into place for this was the second time that the year 1,620 BCE had featured in dating a secret biblical epoch. The first example was with the solar calendar. There must have been something very special that occurred in the year 1,620 BCE but at that stage of the analysis I had no idea at that stage of the analysis what that event may have been.

The next step was to date forward in time from King Josiah in the year 618 BCE to some unknown time into the future. It appeared that this dating of events would also have to use the three periods of 117 years or the three periods of 217 years. I tried the three periods of 117 years and they led to the year 267 BCE. I could not find anything significant that happened in that or the surrounding years.

By applying those three periods of 217 years however it led forward to the year 33 CE. It was again a sensational result for it meant the end of the sacred time line was also the same year when it is reckoned that Jesus was crucified. (This result took account of anomaly where there was no year zero because the year 1 BCE and 1 CE started on the same date.) It was again a sensational result for it meant the end of the sacred time line was also the same year when it is reckoned that Jesus was crucified. (This result took account of anomaly where there was no year zero because the year 1 BCE and 1 CE started on the same date.) This is where a dilemma arose for the biblical prophets or planners may have projected the end of the sacred time line but how could they have known that Jesus would be crucified in that same year? I will deal with that dilemma in the conclusion but for now there were more remarkable details to follow.

I added up the two groups of three times 217 years and one group of 117 years together to establish the actual length of the period from 1,620 BCE to the year 33 CE. The result is shown below:

217 + 217 + 217 + 117 + 117 + 117 + 217 + 217 + 217 = 1,653 years

The result was a period of 1,653 years. Because those periods of 117 years and 217 years were formed from the Reed-777-day formula I checked to see how many intervals of 777 days were in 1,653 years. To my amazement there were 777 days by 777 times to within seventeen days. It was the ultimate in all the sevens and suddenly a mysterious virtual time line seemed very distinctive. It added weight to the position of dating back and forward in time with those three periods of 217 years. It also meant that 1,653 years was a very exceptional time span.

The total in days of 777 days multiplied 777 times was 603,729 days. There was a shortfall of just over sixteen leap days to synchronize that period exactly with 1,653 solar years. This was where the evidence really struck home to show the exact period of 1,653 years was also deliberately intended by the scribes. Those leap days were catered for with two of the most important religious periods in the Bible. Jesus was crucified on the 14th day of the month of Nisan, which was the eve of the Passover. He arose from the tomb on the third day after his death. The leap day period with 777 days by 777 times was just over sixteen days short of 1,653 years and remarkably, the two holy periods with the eve of the Passover on the 14th day of the month of Nisan and Jesus almost three days in the tomb were also in the region of sixteen days.

Two Genealogies

There were two genealogies involved in the planning process by the biblical scribes and these were in Matthew's and Luke's gospels. These two genealogies proved to be an integral part of measuring time in parallel with the solar calendar of 1,650 years, which was outlined in an earlier chapter. In Luke's gospel it referred to 15th year of the

Chapter 6 - The Messiah Immortalised in Time

reign of Tiberius and stated that Jesus was about 30 years old at that time. That sentence about Jesus led directly into a very long genealogy that dated back through the Bible to David onto Jacob, Isaac and Abraham, then onto Adam as the 76th in line. Finally, God was listed as the 77th and last in line. There was a note of caution required for there may be errors and omissions of certain historical names in Luke's genealogy. There were no ages listed for the men in the genealogy, which was a pity because it would have been possible to date the historical event in the bible. A browse through the Old Testament suggested that there were insufficient details about the men who could be found or their ages to try and date event using the genealogy. Therefore, a different method of dating the Bible with the genealogy had to be considered.

An ancient way to date history with the Greeks was to apply a set number of years for each generation. I decided to apply that method with Luke's genealogy and therefore I had to determine the set age for each man from Jesus back to Abraham. It was not difficult to determine what that set age was for there was now the timeline to work out an average age. That average age proved to be thirty years for each man from Jesus back to Abraham. There was abundant support for this set age of thirty years beginning with where it referred to Jesus being about thirty just immediately before the genealogy in Luke's gospel. The Levite priests were thirty years old when they began their ministry and that made a set age of thirty for each man in the genealogy pretty certain. To copper fasten the issue, David was in the genealogy and he was thirty when he was crowned king. There were also three other men in the genealogy who became fathers when they were thirty years of age. Therefore, I took the period of thirty years as a set age for every man in Luke's genealogy. Because it was a set age it created the concept where every man was thirty instead of his real age. This would explain the statement in Luke's gospel where it outlined that Jesus was about thirty when he began to preach. Because Jesus was born in 06 BCE, he was in his late thirties in the year 30 CE. But his virtual age in the genealogy was thirty years.

The next step was to multiply the generations by 30 years and with the 56 generations back to Abraham and the outcome was the vast period of 1,680 years. The period from the 30 year old Jesus back to Isaac at 55 generations was therefore to the year 1,620 BCE. This was an extraordinary result because it was the same as the calendar period in the 4th chart and also with the period of the Reed-777 day periods. It thus was the third hit with the year of 1,620. But equally important it clearly established that the historical event in the year 1,620 BCE was with the birth of Isaac.

It was then over to analyze the genealogy in Mathew's gospel. It stated that there were 42 generations from Abraham to Jesus. However, it only listed 41 names in the genealogy because David was listed twice. Trying to select a set age for each man in Mathew's genealogy was not difficult to identify. The helpful clue was with David where he ruled for forty years as did his son Solomon together with several other monarchs. By applying the 40 years to each generation from Abraham to Jesus the length of the period for the 42 generations came to 1,680 year. That was the same result as with the genealogy in Luke's gospel. Therefore, the arithmetic had verified that forty years was the set age for every man in the genealogy because it matched up with the 1,680 years from Abraham to Jesus, which pertained with Luke's genealogy. Mathew's genealogy confirmed that it was Isaac who fitted into the time line back in 1,620 BCE.

There were omissions of historical names in Matthews' genealogy and those were Ahziah, Joash and Omaziah. However, with the benefit of the time measurement it would now appear that those omissions were deliberately intended. It facilitated making the virtual period from Abraham to Jesus 1,680 years for both Matthews' and Luke's genealogy.

Those two periods of 30 and 40 years respectively were a set age for each man in the human chain of each genealogy. The two periods both added up to 70 years. This is where additional parts of this unusual jigsaw also fitted into the recreated profile. The two genealogies had the same names from Abraham to David but then they were split apart where the two arms then stretched out in parallel all the way from David to Jesus. David was 30 years when he became King and then he reigned for 40 years so his two combined ages added up to the same period of 70 years. It seems that David's two ages of 30 and 40 years ages were the prototype for the two genealogies.

Those mysterious quotes from Jeremiah and Daniel about the precious period of seventy years now took on a purposeful value.[34] It would appear that all the speculation in connection with the predicted period of seventy years was at an end. The period had not really fitted into the time spent in Babylonian exile or other historical related periods despite efforts by biblical commentators to squeeze it in. Instead, this profiled period of seventy years was the sum total of the time related intervals, which were assigned to become the template units of the two genealogies.

A Divining Rod

Here on earth, there was a paranormal force which even modern day science is still trying to explain. It is an empowering energy whose emblem may have been portrayed as a staff and it passed like a baton from Abraham and Isaac down to Jesus. Jacob acquired it as a birth right albeit where he tricked his faint hungry brother Esau in the process for it was the only possession he

---

[34] Book of Jeremiah 25: 11:12 and Daniel 9: 20-27

carried when he fled from his angry brother to Syria. Years later he used a rod to spike the breeding habits of his uncle Laban's livestock for his own gain. The baton passed onto his son Judah but he forfeited the staff unwittingly to his disguised step daughter Tamer in order to satisfy his sexual desires. Moses carried the staff like a magic wand and delivered plagues and pestilence with the powers of its paranormal force. He used it to divide the Red Sea and later he struck a rock to satisfy the thirsty needs of the Israelites. Many centuries would elapse until Jesus would bear the emblem of the staff or reed as he was tried, taunted, scourged and crucified at the end of days.

The signs of this earthly paranormal force came to light when Matthew's and Luke's genealogies were laid out to plot the significance of their historical tentacles from Abraham to Jesus and vice versa. In the hands of Jesus were the two rods of the genealogies and they extended back in time to join together at the time of King David one thousand years beforehand. Thereafter, the two arms formed into one stem, which pointed back to Isaac and Abraham. This vast iconic emblem had the shape of a divining rod.

To draw the image of a divining rod as the shape of the two genealogies would be just a metaphorical observation were it not for the noticeable clues left for us to follow. This was where its stem was right on target for it pointed to Abraham and Isaac who were digging wells. In order to dig wells, the water source must first be divined. Therefore, the paranormal power of dousing was implied. This gave a supernatural caveat to the whole virtual time line period, which augured well for the mystical concept of the Messiah saga.

The scribes made the linkage with the divining rod more watertight when they included the episode in a treaty between Abraham and King Abimelech at a place, which was called

Beersheba.[35] Abraham brought cattle and sheep and he gave Abimelech seven lambs for the King in recognition that he (Abraham) had dug those wells. Some years later there was another episode about digging wells between Isaac and Abimelech. Thus, that supernatural ability of dousing by the first two patriarchs conferred a divine mantle over the two genealogies. The shape of a divining rod is shown with the two genealogies in Diagram 4.

Diagram 4: The Shape of a Divining Rod

The two lists of names were abbreviated due to space requirements. The image of the divining rod cast a supernatural trait over the proceedings. But it also gives a further insight into the imagination and fascinating ideas that the biblical authors portrayed.

There were other clues given by the biblical authors about a divining rod. The first listing was evident in the Book of Isaiah where it stated:

"And there shall come forth a rod out of the stem of Jesse, and a branch shall grow out of his roots." (Isaiah.11:1)

The reference was to a rod and stem, which is a basic description of a divining rod. This statement about a rod out of the stem of Jesse was the subject of much debate by biblical scholars who viewed it as pointing to David and then Jesus. The associated messages in the same chapter were of teaching equity for the meek and so the link to Jesus was understandable. But in the context of these

---

[35] Book of Genesis 21 27-31

findings, the rod signified the shape of the two genealogies. It was also feasible that the rod was synonymous with the staff that the patriarchs carried.

There was strong supporting evidence for those observations and it was again to be found in the statement with Isaiah:

"As if the rod could shake itself against those that lift it up, or as if the staff should lift up itself, as if it were no wood."[36]

The words of the Bible can often be ambiguous but this quote was plain speaking. A divining rod shakes violently against the person who holds it when they walk over a natural spring thus revealing the presence of water trapped below ground. Indeed, the forked rod sometimes raises itself upwards but mostly it twists towards the ground and draws on the strength of the two arms of the person holding it. Such can be the force of the attraction that it can draw the person down on their knees. Yes, down on their knees, which was the traditional pose of Christians when they prayed to the Lord. Isaiah had made it simple to equate the rod with the staff for he wrote it into the quote itself. He even indicated the presence of some greater force where he referred to the mysterious actions of the rod and staff and observed, *as if they were no wood.*

The evidence was accumulating to suggest that the rod out of the stem of Jesse was describing the shape of the diving rod with respect to the two genealogies. The branch that grew out of its roots began with David where his two ages split into the periods of 30 and 40 years. David was 30 years old when he was crowned king and he reigned for 40 years. These two periods were the set time pieces for the two genealogies. The names on the family tree where the branch began were David's two sons Nathan and Solomon

---

[36] Book of Isaiah 10:15

and from them the blood line stretched all the way down to Jesus. On the other end, the stem stretched all the way back to Isaac and Abraham.

The Orbits of Venus, Saturn and Jupiter

So far four separate methods were outlined to date the period from Abraham and Isaac down to Jesus and these were earthly related methods with the solar calendar and the Reed-777-day method together with the two genealogies. However, three more methods were unveiled and they circumferenced the heavens with the orbits of Venus, Saturn and Jupiter. These three heavenly orbits were inculcated into the solar calendar, which had been paraded as two enormous censuses.

The orbit of Venus has special anniversaries in periods of eight years where the planet returns to the same spot in the sky from whence it started. (These anniversaries will feature later in the analysis.) Four such periods multiplied out to forty years. Therefore, this forty year cycle with Venus would have been mirrored here on earth with the forty years for each man of Mathew's genealogy. The evidence to suggest that this was so was visible in the solar calendar where the numbers of the five sons of Leah in the first chart all added up to 292,200 and that was the number of days in 800 years. In fact, the period was one hundred times the Octaeteris of eight years of 2,920 days. The scribes had left their marker where the cycles of Venus were inculcated in the solar calendar. It was an indication that the cycles of Saturn and Jupiter may have also featured in the almanac.

In order to inculcate multiples of Saturn and Jupiter into the solar calendar, the biblical writers had arranged to have the numbers of the alleged censuses altered by having some devious sideshows where men were slain or died by the plague on their journey through the wilderness. In one of the sideshows 250 men rebelled against Moses. We were told that the Lord retaliated and these men were swallowed up by an earthquake. But in a repeat performance the 250 men were destroyed by lightning. To find out what the scribes were up too I adjusted the numbers in the first two calendar charts (were the two original censuses) to reflect the actual outcome with those 250 men who were slain in the sideshow.

In reality, it meant that the 250 days had to be subtracted from the total of the first calendar chart at 603,550 days and the new total came to 603,300 days. The next step was to add this adjusted total from the first calendar chart to the total of the second calendar chart of 601,730 days and then get the average value to form the fourth chart. The computations were as follows:

1st Chart		2nd Chart				4th Chart
603,300	+	601,730	=	1,205,030	÷	602,515

The final total was 602,515 days and it proved to be 56 orbits of Saturn to the very day. This was the evidence to indicate that 56 orbits of Saturn in the heavens above were mirrored on earth below with the 55 men of thirty years in Luke's genealogy. It was the nearest point that the 56 orbits of Saturn at 1,649 years 230 days could get to synchronize with the Messiah timeline period of 1,650 years.

Jupiter had also fitted into the Messiah timeline and again it was achieved with those sideshows where the 250 men rebelled against Moses. This time the adjustment involved the two episodes with 250 men relative to them having been swallowed up by an earthquake or destroyed by lightning. In fact, it involved two separate groups of 250 men in the equation. If those men had not been slain then there would have been 500 extra men in the second alleged census. The second census added up to 601,730 men and by adding 500 it resulted with 602,230 men. This new total when applied as days proved to be 139 orbits of Jupiter to the very day. Therefore, the biblical astronomer had left an example to indicate how 139 orbits of Jupiter were mapped out in the Messiah timeline.

The planets of Venus Saturn and Jupiter had therefore been configured in the solar calendar indices and it seems that this had been prepared in order for those three planets to feature in the Messiah timeline. I have read numerous commentaries about how God and Moses were merciless in slaughtering men on the trail of the exodus. But that image is now changed forever because the sideshows with slaughtering men were just a camouflage to factor in the planetary orbits into the solar calendar.

The Messiah Timeline

The key elements of the Messiah timeline have been outlined but it is also necessary to show the human involvements at both ends of the epic saga. The saga began with Abraham and his wife Sarah. Abraham was told by God that his aged wife Sarah would conceive and bear a son. Abraham laughed in disbelief. Later, three men from God visited Abraham and forecast that the ninety year old Sarah would bear a son and their descendants would become as numerous as the stars in the heavens. Sarah laughed in disbelief but denied doing so when challenged by God. The men departed saying they would return again at that time of life. In due course, the men's prophesy was fulfilled and a son was born to Sarah. He was called Isaac. However, the three men did not return in the Old Testament to acknowledge the birth.

There was something strange afoot in the details and the tell-tale signs began where Abraham's original name was Abram while Sarah was known as Sarai. Therefore, when God changed their names to Abraham and Sarah, a dual story line had begun. Sarah was a word meaning princess. In one story, Sarah was an old barren woman of ninety. But in the other story, Sarai was seduced by the pharaoh of Egypt because of her avarice beauty. Pharaoh's were considered to be gods and so the interlude may have been to raise Sarai's status to *"on high"* in order to place the sacred time line and genealogies on a divine level. With such tactics, the two parallel episodes in the Old Testament were openly flaunted by the biblical writers.

The events spread down through Abraham's lineage with Isaac and then his sons Jacob and Esau. When Rebecca was pregnant with the twins they stirred in her womb. God told Rebecca that there were two nations in her womb. What we were not told was that overhead, Jupiter and Saturn had come together in a triple conjunction, which was a forerunner to the Star of Bethlehem. When the twins were born the boys grew apart just as did the two planets of Jupiter and Saturn.

That was at the beginning of the Messiah time line and there was almost a repeat performance of some aspects at the end of the saga. In the final landscape the Angel Gabriel told the aged Zachary that his aged barren wife Elizabeth would bear a son. Just like the aged Abraham and Sarah, Zachary expressed his disbelief but he was struck dumb for his lack of faith. There was a familiar ring to Gabriel's prediction with the aged Elizabeth, for it was a repeat performance of the three men from God who had predicted that the aged Sarah would give birth to a son. Gabriel later visited a young single virgin named Mary and declared that she would bear the most important infant in the Bible.

Mary somehow became pregnant from *"on high"* and this Immaculate Conception and this was explained away as occurring by divine intervention. She visited her cousin Elizabeth who was then six months pregnant. The baby stirred in Elizabeth's womb, which was somewhat similar to what happened to Rebecca many centuries beforehand. Mary went home after staying with her cousin for three months and six months later Jesus was born. The three men from God had told Abraham and Sarah that they would return at that time of life. However, they did not return for the birth of Isaac. But three astrologers did come to visit the last in the sacred time line with the baby Jesus because they had seen his star in the East.

That was the script at both ends of the Messiah timeline and it puts human faces to the epic saga. The component parts of the Messiah timeline have been outlined and now they can be summarized and then assembled to join both ends of the saga together. There was the solar calendar of 1,650 years and it dated events back in time from the thirty year old Jesus in 30 CE to the year 1,620 BCE. There were the segments of 117 years and 217 years of the Reed-777 day formula and its period of 777 days by 777 times also dated back to the same year of 1,620 BCE. It ended in the year 33 CE, and this happened to be possibly the year when Jesus was crucified. The next method for measuring out the timeline was with the genealogy in Luke's gospel and it also hit the target of 1,620 BCE. Importantly, it identified the notable event of that year was the birth of Isaac. Matthews's genealogy complimented the findings with Luke where it led to the same era as when Isaac lived.

The star of Bethlehem had been identified as a triple conjunction of Jupiter of Saturn in the constellation of Pieces in the year 7 BCE. Those triple conjunctions in Pieces occur every 794.4 years. Therefore, the previous triple conjunction would have been in 801 BCE and the one before that in 1,595 BCE. On checking Luke's genealogy, it revealed that the twins Jacob and Esau were born on the virtual timeline very close to that year. This led credence to the prediction by Balaam that a star would rise out of Jacob for it not only applied to Jesus at Bethlehem but also to Jacob himself and also Esau. Furthermore, it was the same type triple conjunction of Jupiter and Saturn in Pieces at the time of Jacob.

The final display of the Messiah Timeline is shown below in Diagram 5.

Diagram 5: The Complete Picture with the Messiah Timeline

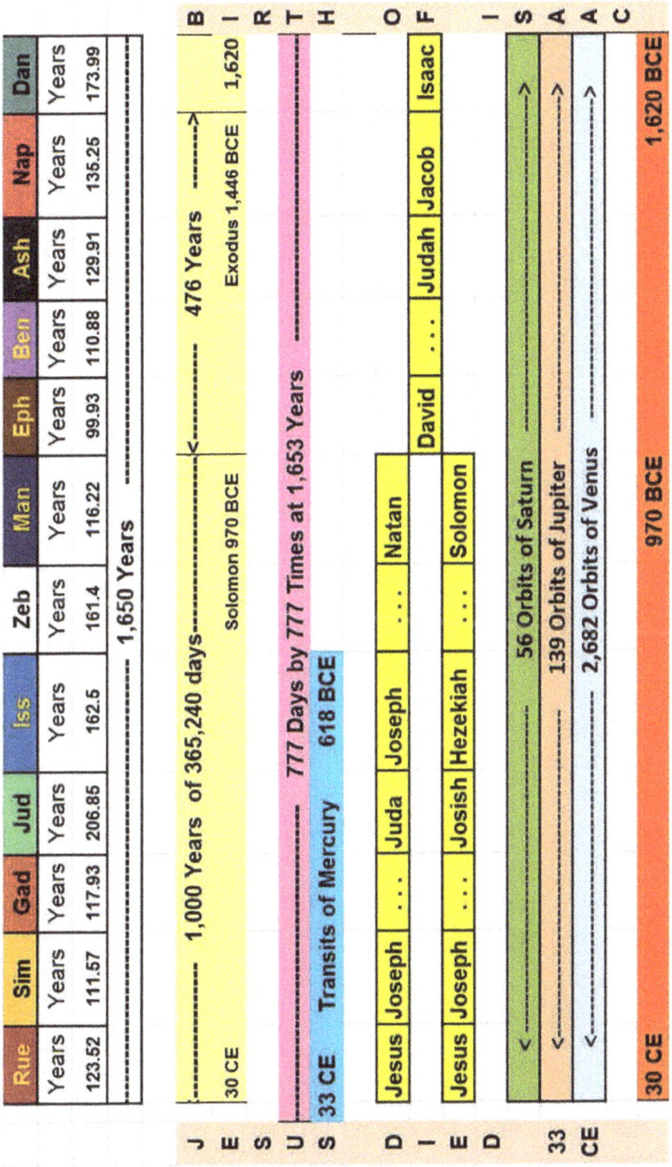

	Rue	Sim	Gad	Jud	Iss	Zeb	Man	Eph	Ben	Ash	Nap	Dan
A	Years 123.52	Years 111.57	Years 117.93	Years 206.85	Years 162.5	Years 161.4	Years 116.22	Years 99.93	Years 110.88	Years 129.91	Years 135.25	Years 173.99

1,650 Years

B — JESUS 30 CE — 1,000 Years of 365,240 days — Solomon 970 BCE — 476 Years — Exodus 1,446 BCE — BIRTH 1,620

C — TRANSITS OF MERCURY — 777 Days by 777 Times at 1,653 Years

D — DIES 33 CE — 618 BCE

E — Jesus | Joseph | ... | Juda | ... | Joseph | ... | Natan | David | ... | Judah | Jacob | Isaac

F — Jesus | Joseph | ... | Joseph | Josish | Hezekiah | ... | Solomon

G — 56 Orbits of Saturn
H — 139 Orbits of Jupiter
J — 33 CE — 2,682 Orbits of Venus

K — 30 CE — 970 BCE — 1,620 BCE

Chapter 6 - The Messiah Immortalised in Time

The details are listed from A to J and are as follows:

A. The twelve segment periods of the calendar and these are listed from Reuben to Dan in accordance with the reorganised tribal names whose numbers formed the solar calendar. The calendar period stretched out over 1,650 years.

B. The periods in years from the thirty-year-old Jesus in 30 CE back to the birth of Isaac in the year 1,620 BCE. The period is sub-divided to include the 1,000 years from 30 CE back to when Solomon became king and thereafter with the 476 years back to the exodus in 1,446 BCE.

C. The 777 day by 777 times reed timeline and it spanned the period from the birth of Isaac in 1,620 BCE to the year 33 CE. It was a total of 1,653 years for the Messiah timeline.

D. The transits of Mercury across the face of the sun were the anchor period in the heavens because it set the particular years for the timeline. The transit of Mercury across the face of the sun occurred on October 11th 618 BCE and it was the likely date the biblical writers used to set the book launch by Josiah. From 618 BCE there were three periods of 217 years bringing the timeline to 33 CE. That was also the year that Mercury crossed the face of the sun.

E. Luke's genealogy introduced the virtual concept of the timeline with each of the fifty-five generations from the thirty-year-old Jesus in 30 CE back to Isaac in the year 1,620 BCE. Each man in the genealogy was assigned the period of 30 years and hence the concept of a virtual timeline.

F. Matthew's genealogy with each of the forty-one generations from the thirty-year-old Jesus back to Isaac in the vicinity of 1,620 BCE. Each man in the genealogy was assigned the period of 40 years and this again brought in the concept of a virtual timeline.[37]

G. The display shows 56 orbits of Saturn from 1,620 BCE to 30 CE.

H. The display shows 139 0rbits of Jupiter from 1,620 BCE to 30 CE. Within the displays with Saturn and Jupiter were the triple conjunctions in 1,595, 801 and 7 BCE.

J. The display shows 2,682 orbits of Venus from 1,620 BCE to 30 CE.

K. The complete timeline from 30 CE to 1,620 BCE with a year zero added in.

The prophets had been meticulous where they had laid down the Messiah timeline with the 4th calendar chart. They set the anchor year on earth by saying it was the 15th year of the emperor Tiberius when John began to preach. It was reckoned by historians that the 15th year of Tiberius was the year 29 CE. Jesus was six months younger than John and the sums suggest that he began his ministry in the year 30 CE. From the year 30 CE the timeline stretched

---

[37] There was one of the forty-year generations, which was split in two where Judah's sons were skipped in place of a son named Perez who was fathered by Judah and his step daughter Tamar. (Genesis Chapter 38)

Chapter 6 - The Messiah Immortalised in Time

back one thousand years to Solomon when he became king in 970 BCE. From there it stretched back over the period of 476 years to the exodus in 1,446 BCE. It continued from there to 1,620 BCE.

Running in parallel with the solar calendar was the 777 days by 777 times method to complete the full period of 1,653 years. One of the most important parts of the timeline was with the transits of Mercury across the face of the sun because it set the anchor points in the heavens to date the events on earth with the calendar. It set the year 618 BCE as the possible implementation date when the calendar was superimposed on biblical history. It enabled me to track the time line back in time to 1,620 BCE and forward in time to what we now know as the year 33 CE.

The scribes had ensured that the calendar timeline of the Messiah was above reproach where they factored in seven separate methods to measure out the lengthy period of biblical history. These included heavenly time with multiple orbits of Saturn, Jupiter and Venus. It would appear that the 29 ½ year cycle of Saturn in the heavens was mirrored here on earth by the 30 year period of each man in Luke's genealogy. It was similar with the 40 year period as the age of each man in Mathew's genealogy for it appears that it mirrored a special 40 year cycle of Venus in the heavens. Within the various configurations were the indices of the Star of Bethlehem and the figures showed that spectacle was a triple conjunction of Jupiter and Saturn in Pieces in the year 7 BCE. From the cosmic data it was possible to form the opinion that Jesus was born as the 26th February in the year 6 BCE.

The Divine Mission

Sometime after the birth of Jesus the holy family had to flee to Egypt in order for the child to escape the slaughter of all infant boys under two years of age by King Herod's forces. Little is known about Jesus after that until he got lost in the temple for three days. Thereafter, he disappeared off the landscape until he began to preach when he was about thirty years of age. His message was radical and it too had been forecast by the prophets where it was referred to in Chapter 35 of the Book of Isaiah and also in Psalm 22. The details were as follows: *"This saviour would preach to administer true justice, encourage his followers to show mercy and compassion to one another, not oppress the widow or the fatherless, the alien or the poor. He would judge between many peoples and would settle disputes for strong nations far and wide. The people would beat their swords into ploughshares and nations would not take up sword against nation."*

We can glean from those simple phrases that the prophets were setting the political and theological agenda for the Messiah where peace and justice would be fostered as a philosophy among peoples and nations. Therefore, it was not pitched for a short term solution but instead this leader would announce a philosophy, which would permeate through time and expand to all territories. Unlike the Greek philosophers with Aristotle and Plato et al, the biblical prophets did not write an open discourse on their altruistic projections. This was understandable because their audience were illiterate shepherds and herders. Therefore, the Messiah would use the art of storytelling with parables to broadcast the new philosophy. When writing was the privilege of the elite, storytelling was the method of mass communication for the illiterate families and tribes and it prevailed successfully over time and space.

Chapter 6 - The Messiah Immortalised in Time

From the gospels we can see that this philosophy took centre stage when Jesus was preaching and we can only assume that a briefcase of tutorials from the prophets was awaiting him. He must have been tutored like a student from childhood because we were told that he amazed the elders in the temple with his wisdom, even though he was only twelve years of age. It can be presumed that he continued his higher level of education until he had reached the age to fulfil his ministry. His philosophical achievements were reflected in the recordings throughout the gospel stories.

These were the philosophical traits of the predicted prodigy but there were also detailed accounts given of his personal life. *"He would come riding into Jerusalem on a donkey and later be rejected and betrayed by a friend for thirty pieces of silver. He would be mocked and laughed at and numbered with his transgressors. They would cast lots for his clothes but not a bone would be broken even though his body would be pierced."*

The radical teachings by Jesus did not endear him to the Jewish establishment. A plot was hatched by the chief priests and Jesus was arrested in the garden of Gethsemane. He was brought before the chief priests for interrogation and to the Roman governor for trial. When Jesus was a prisoner, he was scourged at a pillar and then the guards set a crown of thorns upon his head and strangely placed a reed or staff in his hand.[38] The reed or staff was a strange implement to give to a prisoner especially as it could be construed to be a weapon. Whether it was a reed or a staff was equally important in the final part of the episode. The reed would have signified the Reed 777-day formula in the Messiah timeline. The staff would have signified how the baton was passed on from Abraham, Isaac, Jacob, Judah

---

[38] Matthew 27: 29

and Tamar down the genealogies of the Messiah timeline and onto Jesus.

Jesus was sentenced to be crucified on a cross. As he lay dying on the cross, he cried out in a loud voice saying *"My God my God why hast thy forsaken me. And one of them who stood there took a sponge and filled it with vinegar and placed it on a reed and gave it to Jesus to drink."*[39] It was the end of the Messiah timeline and the gospel writers had indicated the final moment by placing the reed to signify the Reed-777 day formula beneath the last breath of Jesus just before he yielded up his ghost.

---

[39] Matthew 27:46-48

Chapter 7

The Heaven on Earth Configuration of the Tabernacle

    The tabernacle was one of the most holy shrines of Hebrew worship but now there is evidence to suggest that the iconic structure was used by the gospel writers in place of the tomb when they reported on the events of the resurrection of Jesus several decades later. This mobile temple comprised of a tent, which was divided into two rooms by a veil. One room was God's Holy of Holies chamber and it symbolized heaven. It housed the Ark of the Covenant, God's throne and two angelic cherubim. Only the high priest could enter into the holy of holies chamber and that was just once a year on the Day of Atonement. The second room in the tent was known as the Holy Place and in it were a table, incense altar and candlesticks. It was in the holy place where the regular priests ministered and it symbolized this earthly world. There was a fence built of pillars and curtains all around the tent.

    The facts and figures to build the tabernacle were openly listed twice in the Book of Exodus. There was one peculiar omission however where no size was listed for the tabernacle tent. It meant that the various biblical institutions had to work out the tent size. Behind that omission there laid a wonderful secret, which was never revealed by the biblical writers. In what must rank as one of the greatest discoveries from the Bible, it can now be shown that the biblical engineers had designed the tabernacle and its iconic furnishings, so that combination of their various dimensions in the ancient measurements of square cubits had the same numerical values as the orbits of the planets and other related time periods. It therefore had the ambiance of a metaphysical structure and this would explain why the tabernacle was known as the house of God and the gate of heaven.

Nobody had ever detected the numerical data of the planets in the dimensions of the tabernacle simply because the various biblical institutions had worked out a large size for the tabernacle tent. It was only when the true smaller tent size was determined that the displays of the planetary orbits became apparent. The smaller tent size was 20 cubits long, 8 cubits wide and 10 cubits high. There were a total of sixteen planets or related time periods unveiled when the small tent was involved in the analysis. In contrast, there were no planetary orbits detected when the larger tent size was utilized. There were two extra time periods, which were formed from the dimensions of the furniture. The various time periods relative to the surface and square dimensions of the tabernacle involving the small tent size together with the dimensions of the furniture are shown in Table 4.

Table 4: The Orbits of the Planets and Time periods in the Tabernacle Dimensions

	Orbits of Planets and Time Periods	Sq. Cubits	Surface and Square Areas of Tabernacle and Furnishings
1	The Orbit of Mercury - 87.95 Days	87.75	Square areas of the holy of holies, the ark, God's seat and breastplate
2	The Orbit of Venus 224.7 Days	225	Surface areas of the fifteen roof rods
3	Lunar Month 29.5 Days	29.5	Surface areas of the Ark of the Covenant and the Incense Altar
4	Enoch's Calendar of 364 Days	364	Surface area of holy of holies and God's seat and breastplate
5	The Orbit of Mars - 686.98 Days	688.5	Surface areas of tent interior, furnishings, breastplate with veil and curtain withdrawn
6	The Orbit of Jupiter - 4,332.59 Days	4,340	Surface areas of tabernacle fabrics with veil withdrawn.
7	The Orbit of Saturn - 10,759 Days	10,761	Surfaces areas of both sides of all tent and perimeter fence materials and God's seat.
8	Eight years of 2,920 Days	2,920	Surface area of tent fabrics
9	Twice Sabbatical Cycle - 5,110 Days	5,108	Square areas of perimeter fence, holy place, incense altar, table and brass altar
10	Thirteen Orbits of Saturn - 383 Years	383	Surface areas of holy place, table and incense altar with tent curtain withdrawn
11	156.6 leap days with solar time	156.5	Surface areas of ark, seat, table, incense altar, brass altar and breastplate
12	198 leap days of Sidereal Time	195.75	Square areas of tent, seat, incense altar, table, brass altar and breastplate
13	777 Days	777	Surface area of tent, incense altar, table, brass altar, breastplate with entrance curtain withdrawn and veil over the ark.
14	2,300 Days From Book Of Daniel	2,300	Surface areas of assembled tent and fence
15	480 Years Relative to the Exodus	480	Surface area of assembled tent boards
16	The Period of 800 Years - Leah's sons	800	Surface area of tent interior
17	603,550 Days or 1,652.5 Years	1,652.5	Surface areas of perimeter fence and the furnishings and breastplate without seat.
18	A Constellation - 2,160 Years	2,160	Surface areas of Perimeter curtain and external tent areas with tent curtain withdrawn

Chapter 7 - The Heaven on Earth Configuration of the Tabernacle

After possibly three thousand years this wonderful knowledge has been unveiled and it throws open the flood gates of the Bible to reveal some of its inner hidden secrets. It was a marvelous display of cosmic knowledge in the tabernacle together with a spectacular feat in engineering design in the structure itself. Because the discovery is from the most scrutinized book in history, the findings are sure to be met with gasps of disbelief. But the facts are all there and the details are outlined with tables of engineering figures and the relevant cosmic data in my book *"the Mystery of the Tabernacle."*[40] It is important to stress the absolute validity of the facts and figures in this discovery because the tabernacle has proved to be the foundations of a metaphysical structure, which has wider implications for unravelling other biblical mysteries.

Hints and Clues about the Cosmic Tabernacle

The scribes did try to tell us of the cosmic data in the tabernacle where in the Books of Enoch and Revelation they gave hints and clues of the stars but unfortunately these got lost in heaven and hell innuendos. The story line outlined how Enoch had dream visions where he saw a house whose roof was like the path to the stars and he also saw another house with the Lord sitting on a throne and there were cherubim in the scene.[41] How similar Enoch's vision was with the planetary orbits overlaid on the surface and square areas of the two rooms in the tabernacle tent. The scene was like God sitting in his holiest chamber between the two cherubim.

There was also a very obvious clue about the planets in the tabernacle where it referred in Enoch to the seven

---

[40] Michael Hearns, The Mystery of the Tabernacle, www.sevenbiblewonders.com
[41] Book of Enoch Chapter 14:8-25

stars and stated: *"This place at the end of heaven and earth: this has become a prison for the stars of the hosts of heaven."*[42] The tabernacle was a heaven on earth structure and as it said in Enoch, the seven stars were imprisoned or *'bound up'* in what we now know was its dimensions.

This discovery with the sun, moon and stars overlaid on the tabernacle dimensions changed the whole image of the holy structure for it could now be viewed as a metaphysical dominion here on earth. This had far-reaching implications for it suggested that the tabernacle may have been prepared by the prophets to be an amphitheatre to explain in mortal terms their imagery of a gateway from the earthly world of the holy place to the mystical world of heaven in the hereafter as depicted by God's holy of holies place. The cosmic array shone a completely new light at what happened when the veil of the tabernacle was rent in two at the death of Jesus on the cross.

The Tabernacle was a Metaphor for the Tomb

There was a very good reason for why the cosmic data was overlaid on the dimensions of the tabernacle. It enabled the gospel writers to report the story of the resurrection of Jesus in a heaven and earth environment where the used the holy structure as an image for the tomb. This will come as a shock surprise to the readers but the evidence will be laid out to confirm its validity. The gospel writers did give some important clues to indicate that the events of the resurrection of Jesus were told through the lens of the tabernacle. It stated in the gospels that the veil of the temple was rent in two when Jesus died on the cross. (Mathew 27:51) When the veil of the tabernacle was rent in two it gave an explanation for how the spirit of Jesus could

---

[42] Enoch Chapter 18:14

Chapter 7 - The Heaven on Earth Configuration of the Tabernacle

pass over from the Holy Place representing earth into God's Holy of Holies representing heaven.

In Chapter 9 of the Book of Hebrews it gave a loaded clue about Jesus having entered the tabernacle. The statement was as follows: *"he entered in once into the holy place, having obtained eternal redemption for us."* (Hebrews 9:12) He entered into the holy place and that was clearly identifiable with the outer room of the tabernacle. The eternal redemption for us was through the death of Jesus and it was then that the veil of the tabernacle was torn in two.

The theme continued where it outlined that *"For Christ is not entered into the holy places made with hands, which are the figures of the true; but into heaven itself, now to appear in the presence of God for us:"* (Hebrews 9:24) The holy places made with hands, which are the figures of the true now has a literal meaning. It qualified the metaphysical dimension of the tabernacle where the figures or numbers of the planetary orbits were overlaid on its structure. The statement outlined how Christ had entered into heaven itself and this had traditionally been understood as the divine paradise in the sky. But now it can be seen as the holy of holies chamber in the tabernacle.

The theme was repeated where it stated *"Christ being come an high priest of good things to come, by a greater and more perfect tabernacle, not made with hands, that is to say, not of this building;"* (Hebrews 9:11) A more perfect tabernacle not made with hands and Christ as a high priest now served a relevant purpose. Without the knowledge of the cosmic display in the dimensions of the structure, it could be readily assumed that the perfect tabernacle was the body of Christ. But it can now be seen that *the perfect tabernacle not made with hands* was more likely to have been the metaphysical dominion of the tabernacle where the heavenly orbits were on display. The position of high priest was also brought into the picture where it pertained to Christ himself.

There was a very unusual reference where it stated in the text as follows: "*It was therefore necessary that the patterns of things in the heavens should be purified with these.*" (Hebrews 9:23) The main pattern of things in the heavens was the planetary orbits, whose movements are as regular as clockwork. We now know those orbits were overlaid on the dimensions of the tabernacle. However, a new mystery had been introduced for what did the reference to *should be purified* mean in the context of the planets in the heavens?

The Theatre of Purification

At first it seemed to me that the designers of the tabernacle had zealously taken the heavenly aspect to the extreme when they factored in the orbits of the planets into its dimensions. But that unusual sentence in the Book of Hebrews where it stated in the text about *the pattern of things in the heavens being purified* introduced a mysterious new element into the investigation. It therefore was necessary to see what the planets had to do with being *purified*.

I continued the investigation and it led me to the Dead Sea Scrolls where I discovered that the orbits of the luminaries were of special interest to the Essenes. This was outlined by VanderKam where he stated: "*The calendars, with their unalterable rhythms, also expressed the theological or philosophical conviction that the courses of the luminaries, and the cycles of festivals and priestly duties operated in a cosmic harmony imposed upon them by the creator God.*"[43] The calendar that VanderKam had referred to was Enoch's 364 day solar calendar year for the scrolls had revealed how the priests organized their ceremonial rosters in accord with that solar almanac. It was noticeable that VanderKam referred to the

---

[43] Calendars in the Dead Sea Scrolls, James VanderKam, Routledge, London, USA and Canada, 1998, p 112.

unalterable rhythms with respect to the courses of the luminaries, which was similar to the pattern of things in the heavens as cited in the Book of Hebrews.

I came across the Dead Sea scroll 4Q319 and it outlined where the priestly duties were held in harmony with conjunctions. Wise commented on the conjunctions as follows: *"The author thus calculates the number of conjunctions that fall on the sabbatical years."*[44] The conjunction occurred on some sabbatical periods of seven years in what Wise referred to as *"a sort of an algorithm that he (the scroll author) never explains."* On Fragment 1 column 5 of 4Q319 it also referred to a conjunction in the year after the Sabbath year, which was the eight year. Therefore, conjunctions in both the seventh and the eight year were referred to in 4Q319 and these anniversaries were seen as cycles of priestly festivals.

The research progressed from there when I checked on the Internet and found that the seven year conjunction involved the planet Mercury. This planet crosses the face of the sun in irregular periods of seven years to form a mini eclipse in what is known as a transit of Mercury.[45] I also found that Venus had its own conjunction in what is known as a *"transit of Venus"* where that planet crosses the face of the sun in two successive periods of eight years and this happens around every one hundred years. This accounted for both conjunctions, which were referred to on the 4Q319 scroll and it may have been the absent algorithm that Wise had referred too.

The finding with Mercury was sensational because of what I had discovered in the layout of the tabernacle. This was where I had already identified that the square areas of God's inner chamber together with the square areas of the

---

[44] Wise Michael, Abegg Martin, Cook Edward: The Dead Sea Scrolls, Harper San Francisco, 1996, p 307.
[45] Reference www.theplanets.org for facts on Mercury and Venus.

ark, mercy seat and breastplate had the same numerical value as the orbit of Mercury. I had also discovered that the square areas of the remaining structure and its furniture had the same numerical value as fourteen years to within two days. Those square areas were with the holy place, perimeter fence area together with the brass altar, incense altar and the table. Fourteen years was twice seven years so that catered for two transits of Mercury across the face of the sun. The appearance of both the orbit of Mercury and twice seven years were laid out like a ratio to each other on the tabernacle dimensions. This ratio somehow held the key to identifying why the sun, moon and stars were overlaid on the tabernacle.

Those two conjunctions with Mercury and Venus crossing the face of the sun opened up a new avenue of investigation on the purification process relative to the planets. It seemed to me that by crossing the face of the sun, those two planets had come in out of the darkness of the abyss in the night sky to be purified by the light of the sun. If this was the case then it seemed to be a cosmic performance of light overcoming darkness, a theme, which was at the heart of Christianity with respect to the concept of good and evil. But the cosmic examples with the displays of light overcoming darkness when Mercury and Venus crossed the face of the sun, was only a hunch by me. It would therefore require firm evidence to justify that those displays with the planets were on the minds of the tabernacle designers.

This led me to see if the other luminaries with the moon, Mars, Jupiter and Saturn had particular conjunctions. Of course, the three outer planets cannot cross the face of the sun from our standpoint here on earth but it was possible to work out theoretically when those anniversaries with conjunctions would happen. On performing a mathematical simulation exercise, I found that the moon has a conjunction every eight years, which was the same as Venus. I also found that Mars, Jupiter and Saturn have long term time periods where they return to share the same day with the solar year as whence, they started many years beforehand. These long term cycles or anniversaries were as follows: Mercury every seven years, Venus and Moon every eight years of 2,920 days, Earth every year, Mars every 79 years, Jupiter every 344 and 1,554 years and Saturn every 324 and 383 years.

The anniversaries or conjunctions with the seven planets were mainly theoretical calculations and so I searched to see if there was any evidence of them in antiquity. I found in a book by Hermann Hunger that these long term planetary anniversaries were written on Babylonian tablets dating back to the 4th century BCE. It was interesting to learn that the long-term periods that I had termed anniversaries, was referred to by Hunger as Goal Years. The tablets had recordings of Goal Years for Venus at 8 years, Mars at 47 and 79 years, Jupiter 71 and 83 years together with 46 years for Mercury and 59 years for Saturn.[46] Therefore, my research was on solid ground for those long-term anniversary periods with the planets were recorded in antiquity and the academic terminology for them was Goal Years.

Let's recap for a moment so that the magnitude of what is emerging can sink home. We have seen how the designers of the tabernacle had factored in a direct equation or ratio between the regular orbit of Mercury and the period of twice seven years. And two seven year periods had featured with the patriarch's Joseph and Jacob. With Jacob it involved a tent as a bridal suite. (Genesis 29) The scribes had obviously highlighted two periods of seven years involving a tent for a purpose. There in the tabernacle was that purpose albeit as fourteen years. I have therefore taken the cue from Jacob's experience to break the fourteen years period down into two separate periods of seven years. The ratio between the regular orbit of Mercury and seven years was a viable demonstration

---

[46] Reference Hunger, Hermann, Astral Science in Mesopotamia, Brill 1999, p167-170, p 202-205.

of the relationship with the principle of light overcoming darkness using Mercury as the role model. But Mercury was only one example and therefore it was necessary to find the anniversary time periods for the other planets in the dimensions of the tabernacle.

The investigation continued and it was found that the dimensions of the tent fabrics came to 2,920 square cubits. It was a remarkable result because this was also the number as the days in eight solar years. This result demonstrated that the formula to portray the purification of Venus and the moon had been factored into the tabernacle by the designers. The purification of Venus brought to mind the citation by Isaiah: *"How art thou fallen from heaven, O Lucifer, son of the morning!"* (Isaiah 14:12) Venus was known as the morning star and Isaiah had named it as Lucifer, which was a name for the devil. It appeared that when Venus came in from the darkness of the abyss to be purified by the sun every eight years, it possibly signified that the devil was banished by the light.

The next hit was where the anointed surface areas of God's holy of holies place and the seat together with the high priests breastplate came to 364 square cubits. This was the same numerical value as Enoch's solar calendar year. It should be noted that it was the anointed areas only, which had featured in this equation. The veil and the ark were omitted from this configuration and this was in accord with the details given in Chapter 40 of the Book of Exodus. While anointing the tabernacle, Moses placed the veil over the ark thus indicating that neither of those articles was to be anointed. And so, they were omitted from the equation with the solar calendar year.

Next was the surface areas of the holy place and its furnishings with the entrance curtain withdrawn and the total came to 383 square cubits. This number equated to the 383 year anniversary period for Saturn. The equivalent of the anniversary periods for Mars and Jupiter were also

Chapter 7 - The Heaven on Earth Configuration of the Tabernacle

unveiled but their presentations were in a numerical layout and so they did not feature in the table above. With Mars the long term anniversary was every 79 years and this compared to the number of 48 boards, 15 rods, 1 middle bar, 9 pillars and six staves, which all added up to 79 items. Noticeably, all of those items were only in the tabernacle tent and it furnishings.

One of the special anniversaries with Jupiter was 1,554 years. The total of the given lengths and breadths of the tent boards and curtains plus the determined lengths and breath of the bars and middle bar plus the length and breadth of the veil and entrance curtain plus the lengths only for the nine pillars came to 1,554 cubits. The determined values may seem to be a subjective summation but they were validated where the same values also applied in forming the orbit of Saturn thus giving the testimony of two witnesses to justify those measurements. It was again noticeable that the total was formed from the building materials, which pertained to the tent only.

Those results clearly showed that the tabernacle designers had factored in the orbits of the seven planets together with their five special anniversary periods into the dimensions of the structure or as specific combinations of items. (There are only five anniversary days because Venus and the moon share the same eight year anniversary day while the earth is catered for by the solar year) It was sound comprehensive evidence to demonstrate that the tabernacle was the theatrical setting to mirror the events in the heavens and mimic the scenes where the light of the sun would purify the planets after their journey through the abyss of darkness.

The High Priest Lets in the Light with Dramatic Effects

To place the findings with the purification process in context, it was necessary to outline what could be identified and gleaned about the traditional ceremonial worship at the tabernacle. The setting for the purification process was when the High Priest came to the tabernacle once a year on the Day of Atonement. The evidence suggested that this visit was at the rising of the sun. It outlined about this yearly visit in the Book of Hebrews where it stated *"as the high priest entereth into the holy place every year with blood of others;"* (Hebrews 9:25) The Bible did outline the duties the high priests performed in the tabernacle. But it was a very limited view of what was enacted behind the scenes by the high priest.

What was missing from the narrative was an outline of the dazzling display when the high priest drew back the entrance curtain and the dividing veil on the Day of Atonement. The entrance to the tabernacle was to face east towards the rising of the sun and it introduced the possibility of a Newgrange effect with the rising sun lighting up the two chambers of the structure. It would have been like a brilliant flash of lightning when the sun reflected on the gold plated walls and the golden ark and other golden furniture. There was also the reflection from women's looking glasses, which were hung on the bronze altar. (Exodus 38:8) Finally, the high priest wore a breastplate and its small square area made some of the orbits more accurate by a tiny fraction. That blaze of brilliance was possibly hinted at with the transfiguration of Jesus where his garments shone like the sun. Peter seemed to indicate this linkage where he said let us build three tabernacles. (Matthew. 17:1-9)

Chapter 7 - The Heaven on Earth Configuration of the Tabernacle

Let us now enact the ritual step by step by the High Priest on the Day of Atonement. He would have withdrawn the entrance curtain of the fence and then the entrance curtain to the tent and then the dividing veil. That was the transfiguration moment of the ritual because it resulted with the dazzling reflection of the sun on the golden walls and ornaments as is shown in the image of the tabernacle.

Diagram 6: The Dazzling Reflection of the Rising Sun from the Golden Walls and Ornaments of the Tabernacle

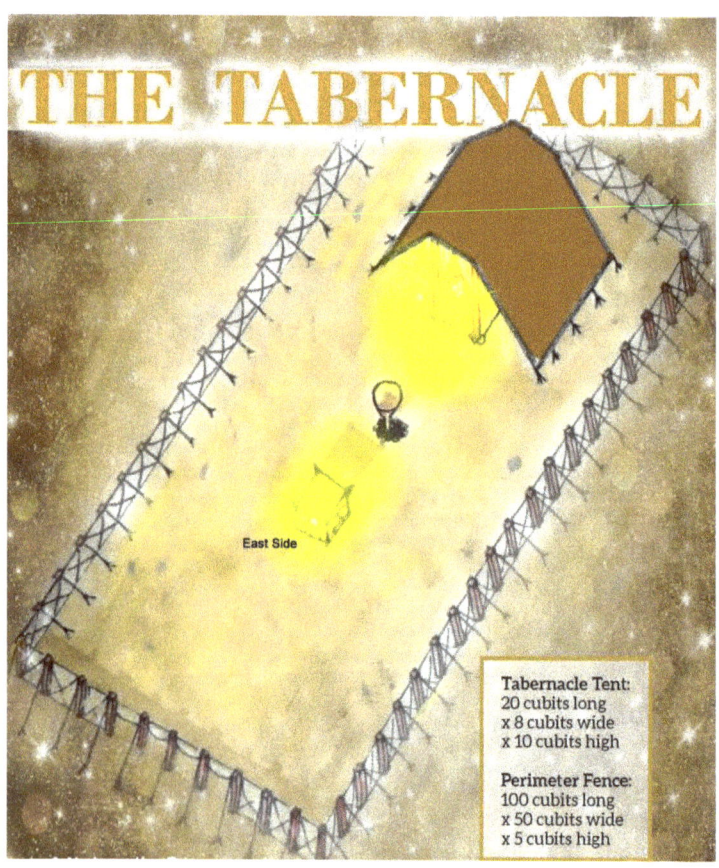

It specifically stated in the Book of Exodus that the incense altar was to be placed in close proximity to the Ark of the Covenant. Therefore, when the veil was withdrawn their two surface areas were close together and they added up to 29.5 square cubits. This was the same numbers as the number of days in a lunar month. The ark and the altar are shown in the diagram.

Diagram 7: The Lunar Month of 29.5 Days in the Surface Areas of the Ark and Incense Altar

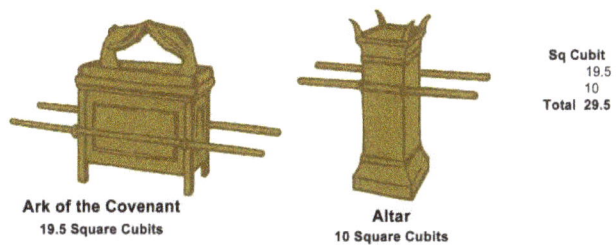

There was a further revelation of a planet where the inside surface areas of the tent walls and ceiling together with the surface areas of the ark, seat, incense altar, table and breast plate added up to 686.5 square cubits. This was the same figure as the number of days in the orbit of Mars.

Chapter 7 - The Heaven on Earth Configuration of the Tabernacle

Diagram 8: The Orbit of Mars in the Surface areas of the Tabernacle Tent and its Furniture

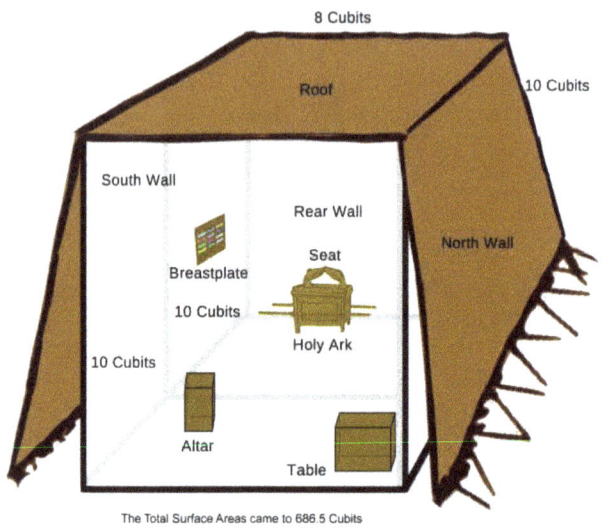

The Total Surface Areas came to 686.5 Cubits

At that stage the high priest would have stepped into God's inner chamber where the ark and seat were housed. It resulted where the square areas of God's inner chamber together with the square areas of the ark, seat and breast plate added up to 87.75 square cubits. This was the same number as the number of days in the orbit of Mercury as shown in the diagram.

Diagram 9: The Orbit of Mercury in the Square Areas of the Holiest Chamber and its Furniture

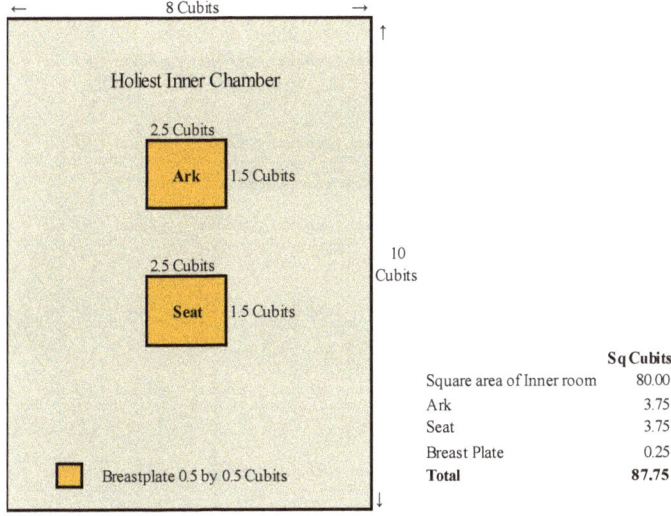

Total = 87.75 Square Cubits

	Sq Cubits
Square area of Inner room	80.00
Ark	3.75
Seat	3.75
Breast Plate	0.25
Total	**87.75**

The high priest would then have taken the veil and placed it over the Ark of the Covenant in conformity with what Moses did when he erected the tabernacle. It resulted where the surface areas of the walls and ceiling of God's inner chamber together with the seat and breast plate added up to 364 square cubits. This was the same number as the length in days of the biblical solar calendar year of 364 days as shown in the image.

Chapter 7 - The Heaven on Earth Configuration of the Tabernacle

Diagram 10: The Solar Year in the Surface Areas of the Holiest Chamber and the Seat and Breastplate

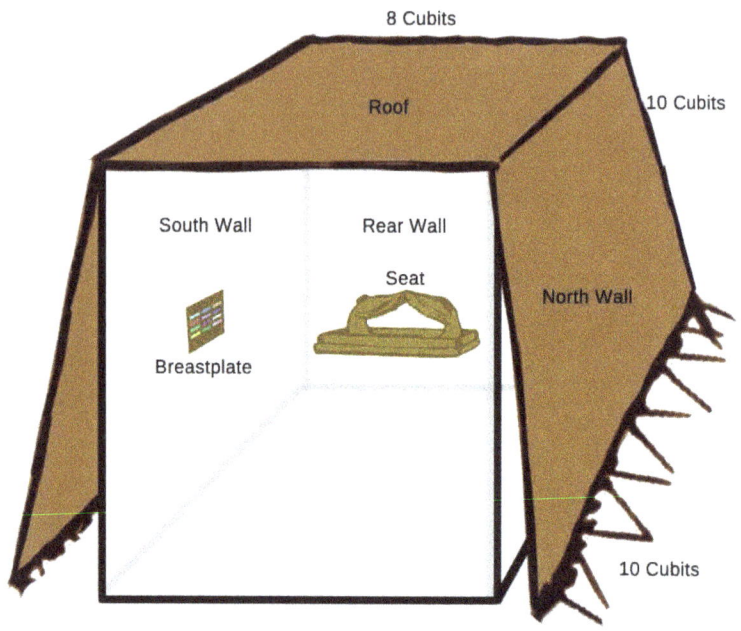

The Total Surface Areas came to 364 Square Cubits

The next display was well advertised to the public for it happened when the veil of the tabernacle was rent in two at the death of Jesus. It resulted where the remaining surface areas of all of the tabernacle fabrics in their pre-building state added up to 4,340 square cubits. This was just seven days longer than the orbit of Jupiter.

The orbit of Saturn was all embracing where it was formed from all of the two sides of the building materials together with the seat. The one thing those materials and the seat had in common was that they were all flat in their pre-building original state or when the tabernacle was disassembled on the Israelites moving camp. In contrast, the ark, incense altar, table and sacrificial brass altar were actual structures, which were not disassembled but were carried on staves.

There were fifteen side bars and but no measurements were giving for them. I found out that they had the same measurements as the building boards. Therefore, their total surface area came to 225 square cubits and this was the same numbers as the day in one orbit of Venus.

That was how the orbits of the planets were formed as the high priest went about his duty on the Day of Atonement. The figures were set in stone and their validity can be easily checked and validated as genuine.

The next display is with the special long term cycle with Mercury with two periods of seven years as is shown in the diagram. It comprised of the square areas of the perimeter fence, holy outer room, incense altar, table and the brass altar. Those square areas added up to 5,108 square cubits and this number was just two short of twice seven years with 5,108 days.

Chapter 7 - The Heaven on Earth Configuration of the Tabernacle

Diagram 11: The Period of 5,108 Days in the Square Areas of Perimeter, Outer Room and Furniture

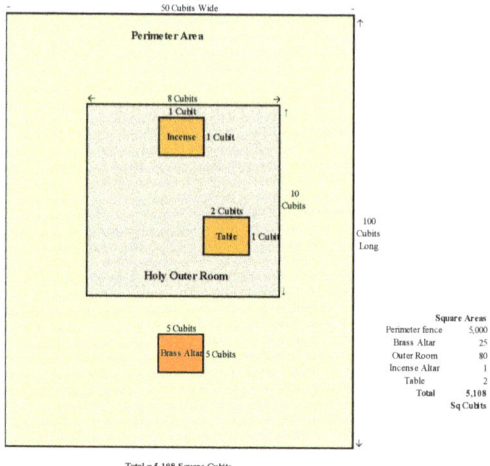

The total surface areas for all of the tent curtains added up to 2,920 square cubits and this equated to eight years of 2,920 days. This was the long term cycle or goal years for both Venus and the moon.

When the high priest had initially withdrawn the entrance curtain, the long term cycle or goal year for Saturn came into view. It was formed from the surface area of the outer holy room plus the surface areas of the incense altar and table and they added up to 383 square cubits, which equated to the 383 years for the long term cycle with Saturn as shown in the image.

Diagram 12: The Special Cycle of Saturn at 383 Years

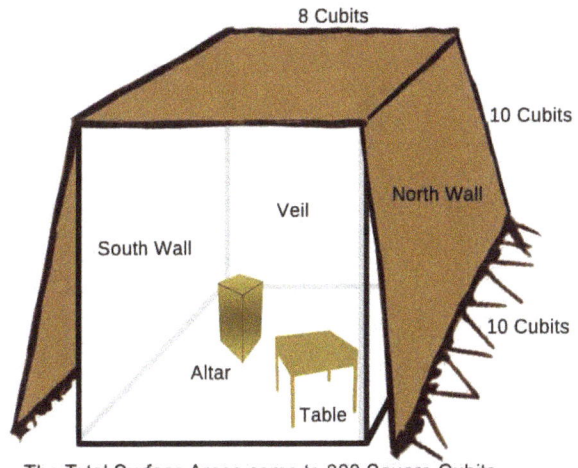

The Total Surface Areas came to 383 Square Cubits

Those were the images and diagrams whose surface or square areas equated to the orbits of the planets and three of their goal years. (Venus and the moon shared the same goal year with 2,920 days or eight years) The remaining two goal years with Mars and Jupiter were found in configurations of the tabernacle. Thus, the seven stars had been purified of their evil spirits or demons on their special anniversary days by the light of the rising sun in this earthly demonstration of light prevailing over darkness.

The next step is to outline the function of the tabernacle at the crucifixion and resurrection of Jesus.

The Date of the Crucifixion

Scholars have tried to date the time of the crucifixion and various years were analyzed from 26 to 36 CE to fit the sad occasion. They two most favoured times were either on Wednesday 25th April 31 CE or on Friday 3rd April 33 CE.

Chapter 7 - The Heaven on Earth Configuration of the Tabernacle

The gospels were very explicit about stating that the crucifixion occurred at the time of the Passover. It seemed as if the writers knew that future historians would be able to work out the exact day and date the Passover fell on. However, the year when Jesus was crucified was immersed in confusion and it could have been any year from 26 to 36 CE. This was where the findings with the tabernacle had a bearing on the issue and it had to do with the orbit of Mercury.

The orbit of Mercury was overlaid on no other than the square area of God's exclusive chamber, the iconic ark, mercy seat and breastplate. Its long term anniversary periods with twice seven years were overlaid on the remaining square areas of the tabernacle and its remaining furnishings. It was already outlined that the planet Mercury transits across the face of the sun in periods of seven years. Those seven year periods are not in sequence but the transits were frequent enough to link them with the Sabbath of seven years.

I found tables of figures on the Internet showing the transits of Mercury back in biblical times. There was a transit of Mercury in the year 33 CE but it was in October, which was six months removed from when the Passover was celebrated. But significantly, it identified the year of 33 CE with exactitude and clarity.

The transit of Mercury occurs in irregular intervals of seven years. But Mercury also crosses the face of the sun in regular intervals of 13, 33, 46 and 217 years. There were two different months when those transits of Mercury occurred. In the first century it would have been either in the months of April or in October. The seven year transit only occurs in October of the different years while the 13, 33, 46 and 217 year transits occur in both April and October of the relevant years. It was remarkable where two of these periods were identifiable with Jesus and a third with the Messiah timeline. For instance, we can glean from the gospels that Jesus was 33 three years old when he died on the cross and a transit of Mercury occurs in periods of 33 years.

The second linkage to Jesus was where the Jews *asked him for a sign* after he had angrily cleared the temple of traders. He said to them *"Destroy this temple and I will raise it up in three days."* The Jews responded by saying it took 46 years to build this temple and you will rise it up in three days. (John 2:18-20) It was the period of 46 years and Jesus himself related it to his crucifixion when he said *"Destroy this temple."* This was confirmed in the very next line of John's gospel where it said that Jesus spoke about the temple of his body. It was therefore interesting to consider what was contained in that encounter with Jesus and the Jews. There were the Jews looking for a sign, a reference to his death by Jesus saying *"destroy this temple"* and also the period of 46 years and it directly related to the temple. Now that we know the importance of 46 years relative to the transits of Mercury, it possibly sheds a new light on why the gospel writers specified about a sign that the Jews were asking for together with the period of 46 years.

The period of 217 years was also remarkable for it was the same period that had featured three times in sequence in the Messiah timeline from Josiah right up to the crucifixion. I had been looking for a sign that might confirm the 18th year of Josiah as scholars had identified it as the year 622 BCE. Now I had found that there was a transit of Mercury in the year 618 BCE. It was an ideal reliable heavenly anchor and it was possible that the biblical astronomers may have latched onto it in order to date the year of Josiah launching the book. In support of this assumption, the jigsaw pieces of the Messiah timeline now fell perfectly into place. For instance, there was now an exact common date back in time, which was 1,620 BCE. It also brought the Messiah timeline in tune with the

Chapter 7 - The Heaven on Earth Configuration of the Tabernacle

general consensus that Jesus preached for three years from 30 CE to 33 CE. So, I set the time line to anchor it at the Passover in 618 BCE. Thus, the three periods of 217 years from the Messiah timeline led from the Passover in 618 BCE to the Passover in April 33 CE. In comparison, the three periods of 217 years with the transits of Mercury led from October 618 BCE to October 33 CE. It is necessary to repeat that in the conclusion, a critical eye will be cast on how the prophets had set the year 33 CE as the end of the sacred timeline especially as it is reckoned to be the same year as the crucifixion.

That jigsaw pieces of the calendar falling neatly into place when 618 BCE was applied as the anchor point suggested that the biblical astronomers had used the transit of Mercury as the focal year to overlay the Messiah timeline on biblical history. This plotting of a timeline seems all so mysterious and therefore we have to look behind the scenes of scripture to find out what was going on. We have already seen that the Torah or first five books of the Bible were covertly re-edited around the era of King Hezekiah and a final re-editing was done sometime after the exile in Babylon. The re-editing changed the whole contents of the Torah where scenes like the exodus were retold and blown up into epic proportions. The new Torah listed sacrificial rituals together with various hygienic customs and laws, which were to be performed by the Jews. In the re-editing process those two alleged census of the tribes of Israel together with the details to build the tabernacle were inserted in the Torah.

The numbers given in the Passover feast that was held by King Josiah helped me to identify that the book, which was found in the temple was possibly the first edition of the re-edited Torah. The re-editors obviously wanted to introduce the new laws of worship that they had written in the revised Torah. Some of those reforms such as worshipping centrally at the temple had been tried at the time of King Hezekiah. However, the reforms fell by the wayside during the long reign of King Manasseh who was portrayed as an evil monarch. The re-editors seemingly had learned a lesson and they wanted to ensure that the reforms would be adhered to in future. So, they arranged to have the revised Torah to be identified as a long lost book of Moses and pretended that it was found in the temple restoration work. Because it had the imprimatur of Moses, the new laws and customs in the covertly revised Torah were sure to be accepted by the laity.

All the evidence indicated that it was the re-editors who devised the Messiah timeline. To overlay this time line on biblical history was a meticulous task of enormous proportions requiring a clinical knowledge of astronomy and shrewd mathematical skills. The planners left an example of how to overlay the time line on biblical history with the total of the periods that Hezekiah, Manasseh, Amon and Josiah reigned at 117 years. It was one of the periods of the Reed-777 day formula for measuring the Messiah timeline.

It would have been essential for the planners to anchor the timeline to a reliable event and the transit of Mercury across the face of the sun seemingly was the ideal focal point. The timeline had been planned to encompass the grand sweep of biblical history from Abraham and Isaac down to the birth and times of their predicted Messiah. Therefore, the planners had to backdate the timeline and they appeared to do this by using that transit of Mercury in what we know as the year 618 BCE as the anchor point. The initial part of the superimposed calendar involved three periods of 117 years and it led to the possible twelve month period when Solomon became king in the year 969 BCE. From there the planners backdated the timeline further in three periods of 217 years and it led to the year 1,620 BCE.

Chapter 7 - The Heaven on Earth Configuration of the Tabernacle

With the backdating catered for, the planners used the anchor point with the transit of Mercury in 618 BCE to date forward in time. The prophets had predicted the coming of a Messiah and they included his full life time on the sacred calendar. They applied three periods of 217 years and it led to what became known as the year 33 CE. The length of the complete Messiah timeline from the birth of Isaac to the resurrection of Jesus was 777 days by 777 times.

It is necessary to point out an anomaly with the ancients being able to see the transit of Mercury crossing the face of the sun. That spectacle cannot be seen without a telescope and of course filters are essential to safeguard the viewer's eyes. Present opinion is that the ancients had not developed telescopes. There was also the reality where the transit of Mercury in 618 BCE occurred at a time of day when it would have been night time in Jerusalem. It was possible however that those astronomers had acquired enough recording from observations of Mercury to be able to predict those transits across the face of the sun. For more information on Mercury and the period of seven years see Appendix 1.

It was necessary to deviate a little from the script in order to place the technical details and unusual anomalies with the transit of Mercury in context. We can therefore get back to the crucifixion and view it through the lens of the tabernacle. It was there in God's chamber that the orbit of Mercury was overlaid. There was also the period of twice seven years and it was overlaid on the remaining square areas of the tabernacle and furnishings. The ratio between the orbit of Mercury and twice seven years obviously related to the long term anniversary of Mercury. The Reed-777 day formula had identified the year 33 CE as the end of the Messiah timeline and the transit of Mercury had also occurred in 33 CE. It would therefore seem that the tabernacle designers had configured the orbit of Mercury and twice seven years in the holy structure to identify that the transit of Mercury was a major focal point to anchor the Messiah timeline.

It stated in the gospels that the sky went dark from the sixth to the ninth hour. However, in Luke's gospel it also stated that the sun went dark. Various theories have been put forward to try and explain that strange darkness but there was only one cosmic event identified and that occurred on Friday 3rd April in 33 CE. It was a partial lunar eclipse and it lasted for 2:50 minutes.[47] But it occurred in the evening time. Perhaps it was the reason as to why the sky went dark and it was almost for three hours, which was in accord with the gospel account. We have already seen that the orbit of Mercury was silhouetted against the face of the sun in God's chamber. The strange thing was that the lunar orbit was also silhouetted against the face of the sun in the tabernacle where the combined surface area dimensions of the ark and the incense altar came to 29.5 square cubits. The lunar orbit is 29.53 days long. There was a message to be read from those two celestial configurations.

The silhouette with the lunar orbit in the tabernacle would have identified with the partial eclipse that occurred at the Passover on Friday 3rd April 33 CE. That would have laid out the date of the crucifixion. The second silhouette with the orbit of Mercury would have identified the year as 33 CE because there was a transit of Mercury in October of that year. This aspect with Mercury could not have featured before now by biblical investigators because it needed the tabernacle in the setting and knowledge of the Messiah timeline to value its importance.

The gospels stated that when Jesus died on the cross, the veil of the temple was rent in two. When the tabernacle veil was rent in two it meant that the remaining surface areas of the tabernacle fabrics had the same number in square cubits as the orbit of Jupiter. There was a tiny error of seven days. The

---

[47] Acknowledgements to NASA at
https://eclipse.gsfc.nasa.gov/LEhistory/LEhistory.html

statement about the veil being rent in two therefore pointed the finger at the orbit of Jupiter and it has been shown that that planet had also featured at the birth of Jesus. The gospel writers would have known that the planet Jupiter was the supreme god of the Romans. It begs the question, had the gospel writers used the symbolism with Jupiter as a supreme god to have the Roman Empire hail Jesus as a king where they had recorded Pilate as writing, *"Jesus of Nazareth the king of the Jews."*[48] The terminology with the supreme god struck a chord with respect to the divinity of Jesus.

    The Star of Bethlehem as a triple conjunction of Jupiter and Saturn had announced the arrival of Jesus. His departure from this world was equally dramatic where the obituary of Jesus was also written in the stars with a partial lunar eclipse to identify the month and date and a transit of Mercury across the face of the sun to identify the year of his crucifixion. The picture was completed where the orbit of Jupiter came into view in the tabernacle when the veil was rent in two.

---

[48] John 19:19

Chapter 8

The Resurrection through the Lens of the Tabernacle

The position that the tabernacle was used as an image motif for the tomb makes it now possible to unravel some of the inconsistencies as reported in the four gospels. Those gospels were written perhaps thirty to seventy years after the resurrection of Jesus and so it was easy to explain away any conflicts between the four writers as scribal or word of mouth errors. The relevant parts of all four gospels will now be outlined to show what appear to be inconsistencies.

It stated in Mathew's gospel that Mary Magdalene and the other Mary went to the tomb. It then outlined how an angel of the Lord whose countenance was like lightning rolled back the stone from the tomb. The angel told the women that Jesus was not there for he had risen. Mark's gospel stated that Mary Magdalene and other women went to the tomb at the rising of the sun and found the stone rolled back. They went inside the tomb and saw a young man in a long white garment. He told them that Jesus was not there as he had risen and he showed them the place where he had lain.[49] The story continued where in Luke's gospel it stated that Mary Magdalene and the other women entered the tomb and two men suddenly stood by them in shining garments.[50] However, when Peter arrived at the

---

[49] Mark 16:2.
[50] Luke 24:4.

Chapter 8 - The Resurrection through the Lens of the Tabernacle

tomb he stooped down and looked in but saw only linen clothes.[51]

In John's gospel Mary Magdalene went to the tomb when it was dark and saw the stone removed. She obviously looked into the tomb because she went and told Peter that the body of the lord was gone. Peter and another apostle then ran to the tomb. Peter went inside and saw linen clothes and a head napkin.[52] Peter then went away. Mary Magdalene stayed outside weeping. She stooped down and looked into the tomb and saw two angels in white robes sitting at the place where the head and feet of the body of Jesus had lain. Turning round, she saw Jesus but did not recognize him.[53] It tells us that Mary Magdalene and Peter were having two very different views of the proceedings at the tomb. It also tells us that Mary Magdalene knew where the body of Jesus had lain.

Those two different sightings by Mary Magdalene and Peter could be readily explained when the tabernacle tent was used in place of the tomb. There were now two notional chambers, the holy place and the holy of holies. Therefore, we can again relate the story of the resurrection but this time will use the tabernacle as a metaphorical image for the tomb in what I have called the *"Tabernacle Tomb."*

Mary Magdalene went to the tabernacle tomb at the rising of the sun and found the entrance already open. She looked inside what was the outer room of the tabernacle tomb and she would have seen the linen clothes and assumed the body was gone. That was why she ran and told Peter and another disciple that the body of the Lord had been taken away. Peter and the other disciple then ran to the tabernacle tomb. Peter went inside the outer holy room where he saw the linen clothes and the head napkin.

---

[51] Luke 24:12.
[52] John 20:6.
[53] John 20:11-14.

But behind the closed veil inside the tabernacle tent, the body of Jesus lay in the inner heavenly chamber. Not seeing beyond the veil, Peter and the other disciple then went home while Mary Magdalene stayed outside the tabernacle tomb weeping.

It seemed that the rising sun hailed in the resurrection and Jesus took down the veil to come out from the heavenly chamber into the earthly holy place, which was the outer room. It goes without saying that he would have put on the linen clothes and the head napkin and wrapped them in the form of a cloak and cowl. He then stepped outside the tabernacle tomb where Mary Magdalene was bowed down weeping blinded by her tears.

After that Mary Magdalene looked in and with the veil withdrawn, she saw the two angelic cherubim sitting at either end of where the head and feet of the body of Jesus had lain in the inner holiest place. She turned around and saw Jesus but did not recognize him but thought that he was the gardener. Jesus called Mary by her name and she responded by calling him Master.

How straightforward it was to tell of the events of the resurrection through the lens of the tabernacle tomb. The picture has told a thousand words and it ended the confusion about why Peter just saw the clothes whereas Mary Magdalene saw the two angelic cherubim sitting in God's holiest chamber. People will wonder why the gospel writers had not told us of this covert presentation with the tabernacle. The signs are that the writers wanted to promote the true High Priest status of Mary Magdalene albeit at some future date when the secret of the tabernacle came to notice.

That is the obvious interpretation that can be gleaned to explain the events on that first Easter morning. By applying the tabernacle as a metaphor for the tomb it cleared up what appeared to be inconsistencies in the gospels. This is breaking new ground and critics will naturally look for more evidence to support the proposition of the tabernacle having been used as a metaphor for the tomb. And that supporting evidence was to hand and it was engineered by the use of the high priests breastplate.

The Purification Process and Mary Magdalene

This brings us to look at why the unusual statement in the gospels about *"out of whom went seven devils"* referred to Mary Magdalene and her only. It stated in Luke's gospel that Mary Magdalene ministered unto Jesus as follows:

"And it came to pass afterward that he went throughout every city and village, preaching and shewing the glad tidings of the kingdom of God: and the twelve were with him. And certain women, which had been healed of evil spirits and infirmities, Mary called Magdalene, out of whom went seven devils. And Joanna the wife of Chuza Herod's steward, and Susanna, and many others, which ministered unto him of their substance." (Luke 8:1-3)

The statement in Luke's gospel about Mary Magdalene and the seven devils also appeared in Mark's gospel but it was after the resurrection of Jesus, which seemed rather unusual. (Mark 16:9) It was also unusual where it was the women who ministered unto Jesus. Mary Magdalene was listed first so she was obviously the leader amongst those women. Jesus had chosen twelve apostles and this number was no doubt influenced where there were twelve tribes of Israel. However, the twelve tribes were subservient to the extra tribe of God's chosen ones, the Levites. It was the Levite high priest and other Levite priests who ministered in the tabernacle.

With the tabernacle as a metaphor for the tomb it showed that Peter was able to enter the holy place therefore confirming that he was a priest. But the women had also entered the holy place of the tabernacle and this was emphasized when they bowed their faces down to the earth when the two men in shining garments suddenly stood by them. Bowing down their faces to the earth was an incorrect terminology because we were told that the tomb had been carved from solid rock. But the giveaway remark of the women bowing their faces to the earth signified that they were in the holy place because it represented earth. It tells us that those women were priests because they were able to enter the holy place.

There was one final piece of evidence to confirm that Mary Magdalene had the status of a Levite high priest and that was with the mysterious quote about her '*out of whom went seven devils.*' This statement had never made any rational sense beforehand and it was taken to be a physical infliction or some type of demonic possession. However, it can now be gleaned that during her time ministering unto Jesus, Mary Magdalene had been ordained to the position of the traditional high priest by him. The reference to the seven devils was the key because only the high priest could banish those demons as depicted by the planets in the purification ritual when he entered God's holy of holies on the Day of Atonement. It appears that the gospel writers had conveyed Mary Magdalene's ordained role as the high priestess using the coded password in cosmic terms as: "*out of whom went seven devils*" relative to the exorcism of the demons of the seven planets in the purification process. There was more evidence to follow.

The high priests breastplate was required to make up the final jigsaw piece of the measurement of the biblical solar year as depicted on the surface areas of the holy of holies chamber and God's mercy seat. The breastplate was perhaps akin to an electric light switch because its square area would have completed the indices of the solar year and metaphorically let the sun shine. We were told in the gospels that Mary Magdalene went to the tomb at the rising of the sun. Its first rays would have transfigured the dramatized scene with a dazzling display of light on the surface areas of the tabernacle tomb. This would explain why those angels and men in the tomb were in shining garments. It was due to the rays of the rising sun. It is time to switch on the light with the breastplate.

There were three main examples where the dimensions of the high priest breastplate featured in completing the numerical orbits of the planets in the tabernacle. Those three examples were with the solar year and the orbits of Mercury and Mars.

Enoch's solar calendar year was the *"burning bush"* of the orbits in the tabernacle because the reflection of the rising sun on the walls of the holy of holies would have lit up the tent to display the 364 day configuration. This reflection explained why the four gospel writers had portrayed all the men and angels at the tomb in shining white garments. It meant that Enoch's solar calendar year had to be activated in order to reflect that metaphysical luminous array.

The completion of the solar orbit configuration together with the orbits of Mercury and Mars required the square area of the breastplate. In all cases in the four gospels, there were none of the male apostles present at those scenes when the shining garments were displayed. But Mary Magdalene was there in all of the four gospels with the men in shining garments thus signifying that the sun was shining. To switch on the solar year configuration, she had to be wearing the high priests breastplate. The evidence suggested that Mary Magdalene was a high priestess and thus she was destined to be the first Pope.

The Gospel of Judas

Late in the investigation I referenced the Gospel of Judas. In that book it told how Jesus had taught Judas about cosmology and he referred to the stars bringing matters to completion. The gospel outlined how each of the five stars who ruled over the underworld had the names of angels. Jesus referred to a star named Sarkas completing the span of time assigned to him. It also inferred that the other remaining stars may also have had particular time spans. The chapter finished with Judas asking Jesus why he was laughing at us. Jesus answered as follows: *"I am not laughing at you but at the error of the stars, because those six stars wander about with these five combatants, and they all will be destroyed along with their creatures."*[54]

This reference to the six wandering stars was outlined by the translator in a footnote where he named them as probably Mercury, Venus, Mars, Jupiter and Saturn along with the moon. That fits in with the findings in my research work where the orbits of the six planets and the moon were found to be overlaid on the tabernacle dimensions. The gospel had also referred to a span of time for the star named Sarkas and there were five combatants. The figures suggest that those five combatants were the long term anniversaries of the planets Mercury, Venus, Mars, Jupiter and Saturn. There were only five of the special anniversaries because the moon and Venus shared the same anniversary period and the earth was catered for by the solar year.

The gospel of Judas was only discovered in recent times and its authenticity was questioned especially as Judas was shown to have been chosen by Jesus to betray him to the chief priests. But we can now see from the references to the errors of the six wandering stars, that the author was on the inside track of the secret knowledge of the heavens. Therefore, at least that part of the gospel of Judas was authentic for it shows that Jesus was obviously talking of the six stars and the five combatants, which were the models of the purification ritual in the tabernacle.

---

[54] Gospel of Judas, National Geographic, Washington DC, 2008

Jesus Ascends up to Heaven

After Jesus had risen from the dead he appeared to the apostles and disciples several times before he ascended up to heaven. He therefore had completed his mission on earth, which was to open up a gateway to heaven in the afterlife. This place called heaven was supposed to be a mystical abode or paradise in the sky. However, it could not be seen or felt by mortals and no one other than Jesus and Lazarus has ever come back to tell the tale of what that heavenly dominion looked like. Instead, we were told that we must obey the gospels and follow Jesus to somehow achieve the eternal reward with God and his tending angels. But how were the faithful to believe in such speculation when there seemed to be no scientific evidence to indicate the possibility of a heaven in the afterlife?

Conclusion

The biblical prophets had the formulas to step beyond the earthly threshold and hold time itself in their grasp. Because of the complexity and magnitude of the facts and figures I feel it necessary to again outline the main features of the discoveries. This should help the reader to grasp the significance of many of the salient points and prepare the way more clearly for a critical analysis on how the biblical prophets could have set the destiny of the predicted Messiah at the end of the timeline.

Those visionaries utilized a prestigious knowledge of the heavens and applied mathematical wizardry to chart out the whole saga of the Messiah and immortalise him in time. It was a magnificent display how those seers plotted out the grand sweep of Biblical history from Abraham and Sarah to the life and times of Jesus. This was the Messiah timeline the indices of which were charted with numbers and written in the stars. The evidence from the calendar charts together with the timing details in the gospels would suggest that Mary conceived on the 27th May in the year 07 BCE at the first phase of a triple conjunction of Jupiter and Saturn. Thereafter, her child Jesus was born exactly nine months later on the 26th February 06 BCE when there was a fiery triangle of the planets overhead. Those heavenly spectacles became known as the Star of Bethlehem.

The gospel writers had left several valuable clues to lead us to those secret calendar charts where they lay disguised as two enormous censuses. The flight into Egypt by the holy family was outlined in the gospels. Egypt was therefore in the limelight and Ephraim was the one to lead us there to his grandfather Jacob when he lived in Egypt. We saw how Jacob instigated the first sign of the cross when he broke with the normal custom to bless his two grandsons. He crossed his two arms to bless the younger Ephraim with his right hand and the older Manasseh with his left hand. The boy's father Joseph was annoyed with Jacob but his father stood his ground and stated that the younger Ephraim would be greater than Manasseh.

The next sighting with Ephraim and Manasseh was with those two large data banks of numbers, which were paraded as two censuses of the tribes of Israel. Jacob who was also called Israel had pointed the way because the numbers of Ephraim were indeed greater than his brother Manasseh and he also appeared before him in the first census. However, Manasseh had regained his position above Ephraim in the second census. On entering the numbers from the two censuses onto a spreadsheet the sign of the cross again materialised with the crossover between Ephraim and Manasseh.

The numbers of the two censuses on the spreadsheet looked ridiculous because almost all of them ended with a double zero, which was not what you would get from population tallies. The writing was on the wall for those two data banks of numbers, which were paraded as two censuses. Those numbers soon proved to be the days of a sophisticated solar calendar. It was also discovered that over one third of the numbers readily converted to time periods, which matched up with the final bizarre ages of Sarah and nine of the patriarchs. Another biblical puzzle had been resolved where the true purpose of those incredible final ages had been identified. They were just long time periods. Their purpose was to realign the segments of the solar calendar by using the order of seniority of the patriarchs.

The next step was to overlay the sacred calendar upon biblical history to see if a dating system could be detected. This would form into a virtual calendar timeline and it needed a starting point. Luke's gospel gave a good indication of that starting point where it listed when John the Baptist began to preach. This was in the 15th year of the reign of the Roman emperor Tiberius. The details about identifying when the 15th year of Tiberius occurred were outlined earlier. I checked to see if there was a celestial marker to identify with the 15th year of the reign of Tiberius. It turned out that there was such an anchor point. Tiberius took complete rule when Augustus died in August 14 CE and notably, there was a total lunar eclipse on 27th September of 14 CE. However, we do not know if the biblical writers had used that lunar eclipse as a cosmic anchor to confirm the 1st year of the reign of Tiberius. Because Jesus was six months younger than John his ministry would have begun in the year 30 CE.

By applying the newly discovered solar calendar there was the period of 1,000 years to be overlaid on biblical history beginning in the year 30 CE. It led back to 970 BCE, which is reckoned to be around the year that Solomon became king. From there is continued back in time by the period of 476 years on the solar calendar and it matched up with the period from the exodus to when Solomon was crowned King. It therefore dated the exodus to the year 1,446 BCE. The full period of the solar calendar dated back to the year 1,620 BCE. At that earlier stage of the investigation, I could find nothing special that might have happened in that year of 1,620 BCE.

It was then over to the reed formula for measuring time in lots of 777 days. The Reed-777 day formula was detected by a simulation exercise and its two long term anniversary periods proved to be 117 and 217 years. Those three numbers with 777, 117 and 217 were then decrypted from the numbers of sacrificial bullocks, rams and lambs in three separate burnt offerings. In all, there were three sets of the merged numbers of 117 and 217 in their particular burnt offering sacrifices. In turn, those numbers proved to represent periods in years.

The starting point for overlaying those periods on biblical history was identified as at the time of King Josiah. It was noticed that the years that he, his father Amon, his grandfather Manasseh and his great grandfather Hezekiah reigned added up to a total of 117 years. It was one of the periods of the Reed-777 day formula. The period therefore appeared to be the signpost that pointed the way to the starting point to overlay the Reed-777 day periods in years on biblical history. With a possible starting era identified it was then necessary to identify the actual starting year the biblical writers had set for overlaying the Reed-777 day periods on biblical history.

The biblical writers had identified that year for us in a most unusual way. In what stands out as the clearest prediction in the Old Testament, they writers told of how a man of God had condemned King Jeroboam for worshiping false idols in the high places. Jeroboam became king of Israel when the former kingdom was divided into the two states of Israel and Judea. He reigned from around 931 BCE to 910 BCE but scholars differ on these dates. The man of God vent his anger at Jeroboam and prophesized that a child named Josiah would be born to the house of David. He also foretold that Josiah would one day destroy the altars in the high places and burn the bones of the priests who were buried there.

King Jeroboam stretched out his hand at the man of God and said "*seize him*." But the king's outstretched hand froze with his finger left pointing. The biblical writers had actually used a finger pointing exercise and it was at words from the man of God. In turn, those words had pointed to King Josiah so there had to be something very important for them to point the finger at. After that the quest was to see if anything unusual happened during the reign of Josiah. Something very strange did happen for it was in the

18th year of Josiah's reign that a lost book of Moses was found during restoration work at the temple. After the contents of the book were read to him, Josiah carried out the words of the prophecy where he destroyed the idols in the high places and burnt the bones of the priests who were buried there. The 18th year of King Josiah seemed to be the target year of the man of God and so it was chosen to start overlaying the Reed-777 day periods on biblical history. But it was necessary to identify precisely when the 18th year of King Josiah actually was.

Some scholars were of the opinion that Josiah was born in 648 BCE and so the 18th year of his reign would have been in the year 622 BCE. The king reigned for thirty one years and therefore he would have died in 609 BCE. But the year of his death is challenged by historians who argue that it was more likely to have been in the year 606 BCE relative to his participation in a specific battle. On checking to see if the biblical astronomers had anchored the 18th year of Josiah with a celestial sign, I found that there was a transit of Mercury across the face of the sun in 618 BCE. I then found that there was also a transit of Mercury in 644 BCE and another transit in 605 BCE.

The amazing aspect about those three transits was that the difference in time between their three respective periods mirrored the same periods with the ages of Josiah. To display this comparison more clearly let's say that Josiah was born in the same year as the transit of Mercury in 644 BCE. He was eight years old when he began to reign and therefore his 18th year would have been in 618 BCE and his death in 605 BCE. The dating method used in listing those particular years was the astronomical year, which is one year less than the biblical BCE year. Therefore, the astronomical year 605 BCE was the same as the biblical year of 606 BCE, which was the same year that some historians identify as the year of the death of Josiah.

Conclusion

The ages of Josiah with the year of his birth, his 18th year and the year of his death would have had to be tampered with and adjusted by the biblical writers in order to mirror the three transits of Mercury in the heavens. It was also the same position with the combined periods that the four kings reigned with Hezekiah, Manasseh, Amon and Josiah at 117 years, which was one of the Reed-777 periods. Strangely, that tampering with the ages and time periods was not hidden by the scribes but instead it was displayed openly in the Bible. This was where it outlined that Isaiah turned back the clock of Ahaz by ten degrees so that the dying King Hezekiah could live another fifteen years. It meant that an extra fifteen years had been factored into those combined periods to make up the total of 117 years. It possibly also fixed the three crucial ages with Josiah in mirroring the three conjunctions with Mercury.

There was an unusual mechanism with the clock of Ahaz that Isaiah turned back, which deserves airing. That clock was no ordinary timepiece for if ten degrees represented fifteen years, then the full 360 degree clock face would represent 540 years. Things got even more interesting where we were told that King Hezekiah had to wait another three days for the miracle to take effect. Thus, there were in all four days of 540 years, which added up to 2,160 years. That period of 2,160 years was the length of one constellation of the zodiac. Therefore, the scribes had not only indicated that the periods and ages were altered, but they had also pointed up to a sign in the heavens with one constellations of the zodiac. That sign with one constellation was possibly to lead biblical detectives to explore and find a cosmic event such as with the transits of Mercury relative to the three ages of King Josiah.

There was also a numerical configuration with the four kings of Hezekiah, Manasseh, Amon and Josiah, which deserves attention because they related to the Reed-777 day formula. The four numbers of the Reed formula were 777 days multiplied by 55 times to reach 117 years to within 2 leap days. Two of those numbers with 55 and 2 were the same as the numbers of the periods that Manasseh and his son Amon reigned. Those periods were 55 years for Manasseh and 2 years for Amon. The total of the periods the four kings reigned with Hezekiah, Manasseh, Amon and Josiah added up to 117 years. Therefore, three of the four numbers of the Reed-777 day formula were inculcated into the periods that the four kings reigned. The fourth number was 777 and it was unveiled from a burnt offering, which was made by King Hezekiah. The burnt offering comprised of 7 bullocks, 7 rams and 7 lambs and those three sevens had merged to form the higher number of 777. The biblical re-editors had thus left their calling card in the era from King Hezekiah to Josiah where they had inserted the four main indices of the Reed 777 day method. They had also inserted a formula with the clock of Ahaz to indicate a sign of one constellation thus inferring that there was also a cosmic influence at play.

That cosmic influence was with the transit of Mercury. The evidence with the transits of Mercury mirroring three of the ages of Josiah was exceptional. It indicated that the cosmic configuration with Mercury in 618 BCE was the likely determining factor with the biblical astronomers in deciding the year of launching what was deemed to be a lost book of Moses. The transit of Mercury in 618 BCE was also the pivotal date to anchor the Reed-777 day periods, which mapped out the sacred timeline. The dating process of overlaying the Reed-777 day periods of 117 and 217 years could thus begin.

During the research work I learned that Josephus had stated that the prophecy from the man of God was made 351 lunar years before Josiah. That statement could not be true because that period of 351 lunar years would have led back from Josiah to sometime in the rule of Solomon. However, it was too much to be coincidence that three periods of 117 years from the Reed-777 day formula also came to 351 years albeit solar years. Thus, the dating would initially be back in time and this was also in accord with the example of the clock of Ahaz being turned back. Therefore, I took the year 618 BCE as the starting point and overlaid those three periods of 117 years on biblical history. They led to the year 969 BCE. This date was in the same twelve month period when it was reckoned that Solomon was crowned king. It was an astonishing outcome because it was the second hit with Solomon becoming king seeing that the same twelve month period had also featured with the newly discovered solar calendar.

The next step was to overlay the three periods of 217 years from the Reed-777 day formula on biblical history from 969 BCE back in time. The three periods led back to the year 1,620 BCE. It was another remarkable outcome because it was also the same year as had been identified by the solar calendar. Two hits from two different calendar methods made the year 1,620 BCE extremely special. But I could not find any evidence to show that an important event had happened in that year.

I continued the exercise and overlaid three periods of 217 years forward in time from Josiah in 618 BCE using the astronomical timing by adding two years extra for − 1 BCE and + 1 CE. It led to what we know now as the year 33 CE. To copper fasten the finding there was also a transit of Mercury in 33 CE. It seemed to be another cosmic confirmation that the biblical astronomers had used the transit of Mercury to set the end of the sacred timeline firmly in a celestial event.

There was still another tantalizing discovery in store and it was revealed when I added up the three periods of 117 years and two lots of thrice 217 years of the Reed-777 day formula. The total came to what could be outlined as 777 days by 777 times and it spanned the period of 1,653 years. The result was like a checksum value to confirm that the three periods of 117 years and two lots of thrice 217 years had been programmed to form the particular timeline from 1,620 BCE to the year 33 CE. That period would prove to be one of the most important of the unveiled secrets from the Bible because it was what I have termed, *the Messiah Timeline*.

The next element of the Messiah timeline involved two genealogies from Luke's and Mathew's gospels. We have seen earlier that the starting date for the solar calendar was obtained from Luke's gospel where it referred to when the thirty year old Jesus began to preach. It was quite noticeable that it immediately led into a long genealogy, which listed the men in the generations from Jesus back to King David and onto Jacob, Isaac and Abraham to continue back to Adam and then God. If there was a way to list the ages of each man in the genealogy then it would be possible to date the historical event in the bible. But the ages were not listed with either Luke's or Matthew's genealogies and the details for each of the men were not all listed in the Bible. Therefore, a different method of dating the Bible with the genealogies had to be considered.

This was where the two methods to map out the timeline through biblical history was invaluable. By simply placing Luke's and Matthew's genealogies alongside the timeline it facilitated getting the average age from Abraham down to Jesus and vice versa. It showed that the average age for each man was thirty years in Luke's genealogy and forty years in Matthew's genealogy. It was an astonishing revelation because there were abundant support for those two set ages in the Bible. To begin with, it referred to Jesus being about thirty just immediately before the genealogy in Luke's gospel. The Levite priests were thirty years old when they began their ministry and that made a set age of thirty for each man in the genealogy pretty certain. To copper fasten the issue, David was in the genealogy and he was thirty when he was crowned king.

Conclusion

There were also three other men in the genealogy who became fathers when they were thirty years of age. Therefore, the period of thirty years was applied for this virtual time line for the men in Luke's genealogy.

It was found that fifty five generations from the thirty year old Jesus back to Abraham added up to 1,680 years. By applying that period from the year that Jesus began his ministry in 30 CE, the genealogy timeline led back to Abraham in the year 1,650 BCE. There was a sensational outcome in store where the mystery of what happened back in the year 1,620 BCE was resolved. It was the year of the birth of Isaac. The year 1,620 BCE had therefore featured with all three methods of this timeline that mapped out the epochs of biblical history.

A similar position was also evident with Matthew's genealogy. The 42 generations from Abraham to the thirty year old Jesus was also 1,680 years when forty years for each man was applied. The evidence to support the period of forty years was also abundant beginning with King David who ruled for forty years as did his son Solomon together with several other monarchs. Mathew's genealogy also confirmed that it was Isaac who fitted into the time line back in 1,620 BCE.

Thus, there were four different methods to measure the Messiah timeline. Those four methods related to how we measure time in an earthly sense in years. They included the biblical solar calendar that was decoded from the alleged censuses, the Reed-777 day of 117 and 217 year periods and the two genealogies in multiple periods of thirty and forty years. There was however three other methods and they were in the cosmic realms with the orbits of Venus, Jupiter and Saturn. This was the heavenly dimension and it cast a cosmic halo over the Messiah timeline.

The orbit of Venus had those special anniversaries of eight years and four such periods multiplied out to forty years. To reinforce the issue there was the period of 800 years of 292,200 days or one hundred periods of the Octaeteris unveiled from the solar calendar with the numbers that were paraded as Leah's five sons. Therefore, this forty year cycle with Venus in the heavens was obviously mirrored here on earth by the forty years for each man in Mathew's genealogy. Next was the orbit of Saturn and it is almost 29 ½ years long. This period was just six months short of the set age of thirty years for each man in Luke's genealogy. From the year 1,620 BCE to 30 CE there were 55 generations of thirty years in that 1,650 year period. During the same 1,650 year period there were 56 orbits of Saturn in the heavens above. This was confirmed where 56 orbits of Saturn were unveiled in the solar calendar.

The 777 days by 777 times of the Messiah timeline was completed and it was short of 1,653 years by seventeen days. That period of seventeen days had been programmed into the timeline with the fourteenth day of the month of Nisan to reach the eve of the Passover and the three days in the tomb. Two of the most sacred periods of Jewish and Christian faith had thus been devised by the prophets to synchronize 777 days by 777 times with 1,653 years.

The prophecies relating to the altruistic teachings of Jesus together with the details of his sufferings and death were outlined in an earlier chapter. It was the end of the Messiah timeline and so the moment had come to enact the final part of the script with Jesus. The gospels tell us that he was betrayed by Judas for thirty pieces of silver and was arrested and taken before the chief priests to be interrogated. He was tried by Pilate, flogged at a pillar and then dressed in a purple robe and a crown of thorns was placed upon his head. He was given a staff or reed and mocked by onlookers. The sentence of death by crucifixion was handed down by Pilate at the behest of the baying

Conclusion

mob. He was made carry the cross to Mount Calvary where he was crucified. The cross was raised between two other crosses on which two thieves were crucified.

The gospels of Mathew, Mark and Luke tell us that darkness descended over the land from the sixth hour to the ninth hour. However, Luke went a step further where he also added that the sun went dark and this may have pointed to the transit of Mercury in the year 33 CE to identify that year of the crucifixion. It was OK for Luke to point to the transit of Mercury in 33 CE because he lived around that era. But how would the biblical planners have set the end of the Messiah timeline in 33 CE which just happened to be the likely year when Jesus was crucified?

Because there was such meticulous planning and all of the jigsaw time pieces had fallen neatly into place, it was highly unlikely that the beginning and the end of the Messiah time line was just a mere coincidence. I am fully conscious that religious believers will say that the prophets were divinely inspired and therefore were able to foretell the year when Jesus would die. But a rational explanation is also called for so let us cast a critical eye on the evidence.

One could write a library of books arguing out the pros and cons of a deliberately contrived plot about the Messiah and Jesus in that role. But the expectation of a Messiah had its roots where the first five books of the Bible were covertly re-edited centuries before Jesus and the disguised indices of the two separate calendars were secretly inserted. This was also the era when the rise of Jewish mysticism with the notion of a heavenly temple blossomed. Therefore, the indication of a contrived plot with Jesus had its origins in a previous contrived plot by the re-editors several hundred years beforehand.

The notion of a heaven in the hereafter was possibly the original aim of the prophets. Solomon's temple had been destroyed and many of the Jews were in captivity in

Babylon. It was in that era that the prophet Ezekiel wrote the description of a new temple. However, so large were its dimensions that it would not have fitted on the hill of Jerusalem. Scholars believe that Ezekiel was describing a mystical temple whose dimensions were written in the heavens. Such a mystical temple could not be profaned or destroyed by hostile invaders. It would be in the minds and hearts of the Jewish congregation and always open no matter where the people lived. [55]

It would seem that the prophets also wanted the members of the congregation to look beyond the finality of death with its terrible trauma for the departing person and their loved ones. Looking forward to the coming of a Messiah who would open up a path to a kingdom in heaven was one way to achieve that goal. That the planners had prepared the tabernacle to be a cosmic demonstration model of how to pass from this earthly world into heaven supported the whole idea of a mystical temple.

The lure of a mystical heaven in the afterlife was similar to what awaited the Pharaohs in Egypt. But the congregation would have to be convinced that there was a life in the hereafter. Therefore, the predicted Messiah would have to be seen to die in order to demonstrate that transition. In the contrived version of events, someone would have to be chosen to take up that role of the predicted Messiah knowing that death by crucifixion lay ahead of him. It was not a happy ending to attract willing volunteers. Yet the gospels have clearly recorded that Jesus hinted of what awaited him when he stated *"destroy this temple and I will raise it up in three days."* He was arrested, sentenced to death and then crucified. Knowing in advance his destiny it would indicate that Jesus had to become a martyr for the cause and went like a lamb to the slaughter.

---

[55] Rachel Elior, The Three Temples

Conclusion

This is where the tabernacle fitted the scene for a resurrection to be staged. It needed someone very much alive to come forth on that first Easter morning. When Mary Magdalene saw those two angelic cherubim in the tabernacle tomb, it appeared that they spoke to her. But then a man behind her repeated the exact same words as if he was the one who had already spoken and not the angels. Something was desperately wrong however, because Mary Magdalene did not recognize the man but thought he was the gardener. He spoke her name and she responded by calling him master. The mystery is who was that man who Mary Magdalene though was the gardener?

There was also the aftermath of the resurrection to be considered. It brought about a new covenant where believers who abided by the new philosophy of love and justice could follow in the footsteps of Jesus and attain eternal reward. It was like an insurance policy and a means of controlling the masses by the planners with a promise of eternal salvation. But it also meant that the planners had handed over the reins to just one man at the end of the saga who turned out to be Jesus. That he could not be around to bring the new movement beyond the hillsides of Judea was another major obstacle in the planning process. But then an enemy named Saul was introduced into the saga and he underwent a miraculous conversion when he was blinded by divine intervention on the road to Damascus. His name was changed to Paul and he suddenly became the enlightened one to preach and write how the philosophy of Jesus should be put into practice.

That was a brief overview of an alternative account to help explain how Jesus fulfilled the role of the predicted Messiah. The extra knowledge arising from the new discoveries facilitated the outlining of a stage managed version of events. In that short overview, the events of the crucifixion and resurrection were not outlined in detail because they involved several pages that would have effected to flow of the narrative but they will now feature.

In all four gospels it outlined that the crucifixion took place at the time of the Passover. The gospels also stated that that the earth went dark from the sixth to the ninth hour. But Luke's gospel had added an extra account on the darkness where he reported that the sun went dark. Was Luke also pointing to the transit of Mercury across the face of the sun, which happened six months after the Passover? Luke wrote his gospel decades after the crucifixion and his account of the earth going dark and going dark may have been an overview looking back that would identify both the date and the year of the crucifixion. The references to the darkness at the Passover could be explained by the fact that there was a partial lunar eclipse on Friday 3rd April of 33 CE. But to be confident of the correct date and day it was essential to also know the year of the crucifixion. Luke's extra reference to the sun going dark helped to identify the year of the crucifixion relative to the transit of Mercury later that year. What gave credence to this possibility was that it was also Luke and Luke only who gave the details to identify the year in which Jesus began to preach where he had listed the 15th year of the reign of Tiberius.

When Jesus was arrested the remaining eleven apostles deserted him and they went into hiding. But his mother Mary and Mary Magdalene were there with him to the bitter end. As he lay dying, he cried aloud *"My God my God why hast thou forsaken me."* One of the attendants soaked a sponge with vinegar and placed it on a reed and held it up to his lips. The reed signaled the end of the Reed-777 day Messiah timeline as Jesus breathed his last breath and gave up the ghost. At that moment the veil of the temple was rent in two thus bringing the mobile temple of the tabernacle into the scene. The remainder of the passion of Jesus will therefore be told through the lens of the tabernacle.

Conclusion

When the veil of the tabernacle was rent in two it prepared the way for the spirit of Jesus to pass into God's holy of holiest chamber, which symbolized heaven. All the evidence shows that the re-editors of the Torah had prepared the tabernacle centuries beforehand to serve that very purpose for their predicted Messiah. The parting of the veil would have also brought the orbit of Jupiter into view from the numbers of the remaining surface areas of the fabrics in the tabernacle. Jupiter was held by the Romans to be their Supreme God and the gospel writers may have deliberately factored in that aspect into the presentation. This was where the writers brought the Roman Governor Pilate into the scene of the crucifixion by saying that he wrote in three languages *"Jesus of Nazareth King of the Jews."* It was a way by innuendo for the gospel writers to indicate that the tabernacle had been utilized as an image for the tomb because the orbit of Jupiter, the supreme God, lay concealed in that structure.

The gospels tell us that Joseph of Arimathea went to Pilate *"and begged for the body of Jesus and he took it down and wrapped it in linen and laid it in a sepulchre that was hewn in stone, wherein never man before was laid. And Mary Magdalene and Mary the mother of Joses beheld where he was laid."* Joseph then placed a large stone at the entrance to the tomb. Because there was concern among the antagonists of Jesus that his disciples might remove the body, Roman soldiers were placed on guard and ironically, they erected a tent outside the tomb. The gospels then go silent until the morning after the Sabbath.

The events of what happened on the morning of the resurrection were outlined by chapter and verse earlier in this book. In all four gospels, Mary Magdalene was the main disciple at the tomb. The details showed that it was still dark and just at the rising of the sun when she went to the tomb. In Mathew's gospel we were told that an angel descended from the heavens and moved away the stone.

The angels countenance was like lightning and his raiment was as white as snow. He told Mary and Mary Magdalene that Jesus had risen and asked them to see where his body had lain. In Mark's gospel the women went into the tomb and saw a young man in a long white robe. He told them that Jesus had risen and stated he is not here: *"behold the place where they laid him."*

In Luke's gospel the women went into the tomb and suddenly two men in shining garments stood beside them. The women were frightened and bowed their faces down to the earth. In John's gospel Mary Magdalene was the only person who went to the tomb and she saw the stone was rolled back. She must have looked into the tomb because she ran and told Peter that the body of the Lord had been taken away. Peter and an unnamed disciple ran to the tomb. Peter went inside and saw linen clothes and a head napkin lying separately. He and the other disciple then went home. After that came the most puzzling aspect of all where Mary Magdalene stooped down and looked in and saw two angels in white sitting at the head and feet of where the body of Jesus had lain. It provoked the obvious question of how Peter who went into the tomb could only see linen clothes and a head napkin whereas Mary Magdalene looked in and saw two angels in white.

The puzzle was resolved when the tabernacle was applied instead of the tomb. It suggested that Peter was a regular priest because he was restricted to the holy place area of the tabernacle tomb where he saw the linen clothes and head napkin. In contrast, Mary Magdalene was afforded the same status as the traditional high priests because she was able to view the two angelic cherubim sitting in God's holy of holies chamber. It meant that Mary Magdalene had been ordained as a high priestess while Jesus was carrying out his ministry. It also explained why Mary Magdalene was given the exalted role of announcing

Conclusion

the resurrection of Jesus to the apostles and ultimately to the universal audience.

The fallout does not stop there because it was outlined in Luke's gospel that the women had entered the tomb and two men suddenly stood beside them. The women bowed their faces to the earth. But there should have been no earth because the tomb had recently been hewn from rock. The reference to earth however identified with the holy place of the tabernacle because it symbolized earth. Therefore, with the tabernacle as an image for the tomb it meant that the women had entered into the holy place. It indicated that those women were priests for only priests could enter into the holy place. The scene in John's gospel completed the picture where Mary Magdalene was shown to have the status of a high priestess because she was able to look into God's chamber and see the two angelic cherubim. As a high priestess, Mary Magdalene would have stood in status above the apostles. She was therefore destined to be the first Pope.

The whole episode of the Messiah had been planned and prepared by the biblical prophets possibly back in the era of 500 to 700 years BCE. Those visionaries had engineered a sacred timeline of 777 days by 777 times and they developed seven methods to measure out that sacred period. It appears that they anchored the timeline with the transit of Mercury across the face of the sun in the year 618 BCE and in turn this set the year 33 CE as the end of the Messiah timeline. The gospel writers had recorded the events of the crucifixion and resurrection of Jesus and had also indicated how the details were in accord with what the prophets had written. I.e., He was betrayed for thirty pieces of silver, they cast lots for his clothing and not a bone was broken.

The writers however did not tell us that they had used the tabernacle in place of the tomb when several decades later they reported on the events of the resurrection. It is from the two displays with the lunar month and the orbit of Mercury against the background of the solar year in the tabernacle that we can surmise that Jesus was crucified at the time of a partial lunar eclipse on Friday 3rd April in the year 33 CE.

How the prophets back around 500-700 BCE had projected the Messiah timeline to end in the year 33 CE when the crucifixion took place is beyond rational comprehension. Christians will devoutly state that Jesus was the son of God who overcame death by divine intervention and the date and year of his death was by divine inspiration. But the evidence from this investigation has provided a whole new dynamic that had never before featured. From that evidence, it seems the whole saga from the birth of Jesus until his crucifixion was orchestrated back at the time of the prophets and what was to happen was obviously relayed over the centuries through an inner circle of priests. The prophets would have known about the triple conjunction or bright star in 7 BCE and that nine months later there would be a fiery triangle with three of the planets. Those were the divine heavenly signs that were awaited by the inner circle and a child was conceived and born in that period. By all account, the baby was a bright boy named Jesus and he fitted the expectation of a divine saviour. Very little is known of Jesus until he appeared on the stage when he was about thirty years of age. The stories about his preaching and working miracles were only recorded in written format around forty to seventy years later, yet they are regarded as '*the gospel truth.*'

There were the awkward set of events surrounding the arrest and crucifixion of Jesus. If he did die on the cross then it needed a different man to be present at the tabernacle tomb on the morning of the resurrection. This suggestion has merit because Mary Magdalene did not recognize the man as Jesus but thought he was the

Conclusion

gardener. He spoke to her and she called him master but that could be her acknowledging a new leader.

From there an enemy named Saul entered the saga. He experienced a divine encounter on the road to Damascus in Syria and his name was changed to Paul. It was like a repeat of what happened to the patriarch Jacob though he was on the way back from Syria. Jacob had also acquired a new name called Israel and under that pseudonym, the re-editors of the Torah made a mass movement out of the twelve tribes of Israel and had them that capture the Promised Land. It was a sign of things to come where those twelve tribes were formed into the shape of a cross around the tabernacle especially as their numbers formed the Messiah timeline that ended with a cross. The re-editors had set the scene for Israel (Jacob) to begin a mass movement that would eventually take over the Promised Land while at the end of the Messiah timeline, Paul would step in to promote the new philosophy of Jesus in a series of epistolic letters that spread to the universal audience.

That was a possible overview of what may have gone on behind the scenes. Those involved believed in a one true God and it was therefore likely that the coming of a Messiah was a divine covenant to be followed with zeal. It would have taken tremendous planning and sworn loyalty to achieve the goals as the meticulous facts and figures of the Messiah timeline demonstrate. How they acquired and recorded the incredible knowledge of astronomy that deified the Messiah timeline would seem to be beyond the capability of mere mortals to know at that early stage of engineering development. That all the jigsaw pieces fell into place is testimony to master minds that were operating on an inspired plane of intelligence. And Jesus was in the right place Bethlehem at the right time to be the predicted and planned Messiah.

The philosophy prepared and prompted by the prophets had borne fruit and the greatest story ever told came true. Despite the onslaughts by King Herod or the collusion by the high priest Caiaphas, the egalitarian philosophy survived the egos of kings and tyrants to eventually become the cornerstone of modern democracies. It was a miraculous accomplishment for the biblical prophets to plan and propagate long before the empires of Greece or Rome were ever etched on a signpost.

Appendix 1: Mercury, Seven Years and Peace Offerings

Because Josiah had been fingered at the time of King Jeroboam, I checked and noticed that the 18th year of Jeroboam's reign was also listed with him. Jeroboam died in the 22nd year of his reign, which was reckoned be in 910 BCE. His 18th year would thus have been in 914 BCE. There was also a transit of Mercury across the face of the sun in October of 914 BCE. The 18th year of Jeroboam's reign in 914 BCE, the 18th year of Josiah's reign in 618 BCE and a transit of Mercury in both those years. I wondered if the 18th year of a king's reign might be a reference point in the Old Testament.

I checked and found that the 18th year applied to only four monarchs in the Bible. Those kings were Jeroboam, Jehoshaphat, Josiah and Nebuchadnezzar of Babylon. The 18th year of the reign of Jehoshaphat was when Jehoram began to reign and it was reckoned to be in the year 849 BCE. This was getting predictable because there was also a transit of Mercury across the face of the sun in October of that year. It should be noted that the astronomical method of dating was used and it has one year extra added to compensate for the absence of a year zero in the original calendar.

The final listing was with the 18th year of Nebuchadnezzar and that was reckoned to be in the years 586 or 587 BCE. It was a very notable time because it was when Jerusalem was captured by the Babylonians. I found that there was also a transit of Mercury in October of 585 BCE, which was 586

BCE when the extra year for the biblical BCE dating was applied. Was the invasion of Jerusalem at the time of a transit of Mercury just a mere coincidence? The Babylonians were known to wait for Jupiter to be in ascendency before they would anoint a new king. It raises to possibility that Nebuchadnezzar may have deliberately chosen the time of a transit of Mercury to make it a bad omen for the Jews when he invaded Jerusalem.

The results with the at least three listings of the 18th year had shown that the biblical astronomers may have had dated certain events in the Bible by using the transit of Mercury across the face of the sun.

It was outlined earlier that Wise had referred to a secret algorithm that the Essenes had used in calculating conjunctions of the planets. That algorithm had not been revealed in the Dead Sea scrolls but from the analysis so far it proved possible to identify its main indices. The evidence suggested that it related to the transit of Mercury and its frequency in crossing the face of the sun. We now know that this happens in irregular intervals of seven years but only in October. The transit is more frequent in periods of 33 years, 46 years and 217 years and in biblical times, these happened in the months of April and October. The period of seven years was synonymous with the Sabbath of seven years and double the period of seven years was overlaid on the tabernacle dimensions.

It turned out that the biblical astronomers had laid down a decisive marker with the period of seven years where they encrypted the numbers of days in that period into the Old Testament. This was in Chapter 7 of the Book of numbers where it outlined how each leader of the twelve tribes of Israel made a Peace Offering of **two** bullock, **five** rams, **five** he goats and **five** lambs. It was back to the eye test where there was another optical mirage in store. When the numbers of bullocks, rams, he goats and lambs were entered onto a spreadsheet the outline was as follows:

Appendix 1: Mercury, Seven Years and Peace Offerings

Bullocks	Rams	Goats	Lambs
2	5	5	5

The four individual figures merged into the one large number of 2,555. This number equated to the period of seven years of 365 by 7 days. It was the period of seven sabbatical years and also it identified with the conjunction of seven years with the transit of Mercury across the face of the sun.

The leaders of each of the twelve tribes also made a Burnt offering of **one** bullock, **one** ram and **one** lamb over the period of twelve days. When the data was entered onto a spreadsheet the outline was as follows:

Bullocks	Rams	Lambs
1	1	1

The three individual figures had merged into the bigger number of 111. Just like the previous encounters with the encryptions of the numbers 777 and 2,555, the merged number of 111 turned out to be a period in days. But this time, the scribes had left the indices to indicate that the large number of 111 was intended because the total of all the listings of the 1st days in the offerings in Chapter 7 of the Book of Number together with the listings of the number one added up to a total of 111.

There was also a possible total to confirm that the merged number of 2,555 was intended. The total of the numbers of treasure offerings with the utensils of one silver charger, weighing 130 shekels, one silver bowl weighing 70 shekels and one golden spoon weighing 10 shekels all collectively added up to 2,556. Of course, you cannot add up chargers, bowls, and spoons with shekels because it is adding hardware items to theoretical weights. There was however one exception and that was with what is known as a mathematical checksum.

A checksum is where all the numbers of items are counted up irrespective of what they represent and the total is recorded for future checks. When the figures are checked sometime in the future and the total is the same then it is an indication that all of the individual numbers of items had retained their original values intact. The checksum total of all of the donated treasures at 2,556 was thus a possible validation process to show that the encrypted number of, 2,555 was intended by the scribes.

The difference between 2,555 and 2,556 could readily be accounted for if the numbers were intended to represent time periods. If the number 2,555 represented a period of seven years, then one leap day would have to be added to synchronize this calendar period with the true length of the solar year. In the course of twelve periods of seven years at 84 years in the Peace offerings, the leap days would add up to a total of 21 days.

Therefore, there was the distinct possibility that twelve periods of 2,555 days of seven years and twelve periods of 111 days together with 21 leap days had been encrypted into the Peace and Burnt offerings using the identity of animals as symbolic notations. But why had the scribes found it necessary to go beyond just one offering and list twelve offerings for each Peace and Burnt offering?

I added up the total of what I perceived to be days in both offerings. The figures were 111 by 12 = 1,332 for the Burnt offerings plus 2,555 by 12 = 30,660 for the Peace offering. Their two totals came to 31,992. The extra 21 leap days in 84 years brought the total to 32,013. This number proved to be the orbit of Mercury at 87.95 days multiplied by Enoch's 364 day solar calendar year. It was the two numbers with the orbit of Mercury at 87.95 days and Enoch's solar calendar at 364 days both of which were overlaid on the dimensions of God's holiest chamber in the tabernacle.

Bibliography

Bible KJV, Books of Enoch, Jasher, Jubilees.

Budge A. E. Wallis, *The Book of the Dead, The Papyrus of Ani*, British Museum, London 1895.

Elior, Rachel, *The three Temples*, the Littman Library of Jewish Civilization, United States and Canada, 2005.

Friedman, Richard Elliot, *Who Wrote the Bible?* New York: Harper, 1997.

Giorgio De Santillana, Hertha von Dechend, David R. *Hamlets Mill,* Publisher Godine, 1977

Hughes David W, *Astronomical Thoughts on the Star of Bethlehem* at https://books.google.ie/books?isbn=9004308474

Hunger, Hermann, *Astral Science in Mesopotamia*, Brill 1999.

Lunn Nicholas P, *Jesus, the Ark and the Day of Atonement,* Wycliffe Bible translators, England.

McLeish, John, *Number*: London: Bloomsbury, 1991.

NASA at https://eclipse.gsfc.nasa.gov/LEhistory/LEhistory.html

Neugebauer, O. *The Exact Sciences in Antiquity*, New York, Dover 1969

The Works of Josephus: *Complete and Unabridged, New Updated Edition*, Translated by William Whiston, Peabody, Mass, Hendrickson, 1987.

Rodriguez, Angel, Manuel, *The Symbolism of the Four Cardinal Directions,* Biblical Research Institute, www.adventistbiblicalresearch.org

VanderKam James, *Calendars in the Dead Sea Scrolls*, Routledge, London, USA and Canada, 1998.

Wise Michael, Abegg Martin, Cook Edward: *The Dead Sea Scrolls*, Harper San Francisco, 1996, p 307.

www.theplanets.org

www.space.com

DISCLAIMER

While every care has been taken in the compilation of this book, neither the author nor the publisher nor the editor can accept responsibility for errors or omissions. Where such errors or omissions occur and are brought to our attention, they will be corrected for future editions of this book.

www.ingramcontent.com/pod-product-compliance
Lightning Source LLC
Chambersburg PA
CBHW051600010526
44118CB00023B/2763